1950
SD

The Double Standard

The Double Standard

A Feminist Critique of
Feminist Social Science

MARGRIT EICHLER

CROOM HELM LONDON

© 1980 Margrit Eichler
Croom Helm Ltd, 2-10 St John's Road, London SW11

British Library Cataloguing in Publication Data

Eichler, Margrit
    The double standard.
    1. Women — Social conditions
    I. Title
    301.41'2   HQ1206
    ISBN 0-85664-536-2
    ISBN 0-7099-0177-1 Pbk

Printed in Great Britain by
Biddles Ltd, Guildford, Surrey

CONTENTS

Dedicated to
GERNOT KÖHLER

who has had to bear the brunt of my personal struggle
with the double standard in society.

ACKNOWLEDGEMENTS

This book has been several years in the writing. During this entire time I taught classes which in some way or other utilised the thoughts contained herein, which were thereby exposed to the criticisms, comments, and above all, questions of my students. Their collective contribution to my thinking was very considerable. In addition, friends and colleagues read parts or all of the manuscript at various stages of manuscript preparation. I would like to cordially thank Linda Fischer, Frieda Forman, Jonah Goldstein, Adrienne Harris, Cyril Levitt, Lorna Marsden, Thelma McCormack, Jennifer Newton, Mary O'Brien, Marylee Stephenson, and Jane Synge for giving me feedback and criticism. I did not, in all circumstances, agree with all the criticisms made, but in all cases it helped to sharpen the argument. David Croom did a thorough editing job for the first part of the manuscript, which was sometimes frustrating, but helped considerably in improving the final product, and Melanie Crook capably edited the last two chapters and saw the book efficiently through production.

1 INTRODUCTION

Feminist research and writings centre around issues of inequality. At its best, feminist writing fulfils three functions: it is critical of existent social structures and ways to perceive them, it serves as a corrective mechanism by providing an alternative viewpoint and data to substantiate it, and it starts to lay the groundwork for a transformation of social science and society.[1]

The processes of criticism, correction and transformation form a logical sequence but not a chronological one. Perhaps the best way to visualise the over-all process is to think of it as a constant going back and forth between the three components. Ultimately, criticism will only be effective if it is able to generate a better alternative (transformation). On the other hand, we will only be able to improve social science (and perhaps society) after we have engaged in a thorough criticism and have gone through the necessary corrective steps. In order to criticise, we need a vision; in order to have a vision, we need to be critical of the present situation. Both criticism and vision need to be grounded in data. We can think of this process as continually going on at different levels.

Feminist scholarship can be seen as having gone through one cycle of criticism, corrective action, and incipient transformation. We are now at a point where we can start the process over again, but on the basis of the critical work that has already been done. This book is located in a tradition of feminist scholarship and tries to criticise not only mainstream social science but also some of its feminist critiques for not going far enough. It is a general paradox of critical thought that a critique remains antithetically tied to what it criticises. In the case of feminist scholarship, the criticism is geared towards sexism in language, in the type of questions asked, in the types of assumptions made, etc. In political terms, feminist efforts are geared towards the abolition of sex roles and sex distinctions. In terms of scholarship, feminist efforts are geared towards the exploration and charting of sex roles and sex differences in order to be able to understand and ultimately to overcome them. It is one of the major theses of this book that in spite of this explicit intent feminist critiques may unintentionally reinforce rather than abolish sex roles and sex distinctions.

Perhaps a personal example will help clarify this phenomenon. Not too long ago I attended a conference which brought together fifty Canadian women who were considered leaders in their fields in government, from the business world, in the publishing business, and from academia. At some point, this larger group broke up into smaller discussion sections. The section of which I was a part started to discuss the failure of women to assert themselves, their fear of success, their inability to speak in public, etc. There were earnest nods all around when one speaker said that we as women did not know how to behave in public, and how to be successful in various types of organisations. The ironic aspect of this was that there was not a single woman in that group who had not successfully made her way against all odds in a male-dominated field, who did not hold a responsible position in a formal organisation, and who did not frequently speak in public.

This is an example of the reinforcement of sexual stereotypes because of research that is feminist in its impetus, which sets out to criticise sex stereotyping and sex role allocation, but which in the process transmits the image that sex role stereotyping and sex role allocation are more omnipresent than is, in fact, the case.

A similar type of paradoxical relationship is operative at the language level. It is a well-accepted tenet that one cannot do non-sexist scholarship with sexist language. If we employ the generic 'he', 'man' or 'mankind' it is unclear when we are talking about all humans and when specifically about males. Using so-called generic terms hides the fact that often only males are, in fact, considered. At best it is a highly confusing and inaccurate language. In addition, it has been concluded that ' . . . linguistic form can be a *cause* of sexism as well as the reverse . . . . (Moulton, Robinson and Elias, 1978, p.1033).

The criticism has so far focused on the use of male terms for supposedly general purposes. Here, this criticism will be extended to the most central term when dealing with sex inequalities, namely to the term 'sex' when it is used as a qualifying attribute. Two of the most important concepts in feminist research are 'sex roles' and 'sex identity'. These concepts are ambiguous in so far as they do not distinguish between social and biological differences and similarities between the sexes. While on the one hand these are necessary concepts for understanding sex inequalities, on the other hand they impede our understanding due to their ambiguous nature. One of the tasks we will pursue in this book is to sort out to what degree and in what way these are useful concepts and when they become a cause of sexism.

To come back to the analogy of sexist language, we have not discarded the use of the terms 'he', 'man', 'mankind', etc., we have merely restricted them to their proper sphere, namely to refer to males. To indicate general applicability, other concepts have been activated: one, they, people, humanity, humankind, etc. Similarly, the task with respect to terms like 'sex roles' and 'sex identity' is to restrict them to their proper spheres as useful descriptive terms which however must not be used as explanatory causal variables in order to avoid the biological fallacy.

The biological fallacy consists of trying to explain social facts by biological facts. Biology is, for humans, always mediated by culture. Therefore, we cannot explain a social sex difference through a biological sex difference, since the *meaning* of a biological sex difference varies according to the culture through which it is mediated. Let us take an example to clarify the relationship between biology and culture in general terms.

In frontier times, a person had a significantly higher chance of being a good hunter if he or she had good vision, could move swiftly and had stamina. Today, when people kill animals out of airplanes, with telescopic rifles, they may be short-sighted, lame, diabetic and obese and yet carry home more game than the swiftest of earlier hunters. The meaning of such biological factors has changed with the culture.

Or, closer to home, men tend to have more muscle tissue than women. This tendency towards greater physical strength in males tends to be exaggerated in western industrialised countries in which boys are much more encouraged, motivated and even coerced to participate in physical activities than are girls. A natural tendency towards somewhat greater muscular strength is therefore greatly increased through a cultural factor: physical activity. In countries in which women customarily carry the burden, their muscles may be better developed than those of the men.

Finally, it is constantly cited as one of the unshakeable truths in sex relations that only women lactate and that therefore women must look after small babies. Here, too, culture has intervened with prepared formula and bottlefeeding. While it seems to be true that breastfeeding is more advantageous for mother and child at least for a limited period of time (the uterus contracts more quickly when a mother breastfeeds and the child receives some antibiotics from the mother's milk that it does not get through formula), the length of time that a child is breastfed can be greatly reduced if so desired and the lactating mother gains flexibility if the child is on a mixed breast – bottle diet.

The example of breastfeeding *v* bottlefeeding is a particularly instructive one to illuminate the interplay between biology and culture, because the virtues of bottle- and breastfeeding have both been greatly exaggerated into the direction of culture triumphing over nature or nature triumphing over culture. Neither is, of course, true. The mother is no longer immutably tied to the nursing child because of the advancement in mother's milk substitutes but, on the other hand, formula does not totally replace all the functions that breastfeeding fulfilled. To what degree breastfeeding becomes optional rather than necessary is a function not only of the availability of the technology but also of the over-all cultural context within which a nursing mother finds herself. Recently, there have been concerted efforts to sell prepared babyfoods, including formula, in developing countries. Given a generally low standard of living, such products are very expensive in those countries. Their costs far exceed their benefits if and when a mother can nurse. In addition, they are highly impractical. As a rule, there is no adequate refrigeration, nor adequate sterilisation equipment, nor sufficient capital to buy the necessary quantities of formula for their large-scale introduction. Given these pre-existent cultural factors, using high-pressure sales techniques with misleading advertisements may indeed amount to a form of genocide, as has been charged (Wade, 1974).

In other words, the relationship between culture and biology is a constantly changing one, dependent on the interplay of many factors. To draw any direct inferences from biological differences – of whatever kind – to social differences without giving careful attention to the culture through which such biological differences are mediated is to commit a grave error.

When we are dealing with sex differences, we are dealing with social inequalities which happen to coincide with certain biological differences. Early on, researchers tried to solve the problem of the confusion of biological with social attributes by distinguishing between gender and sex. Gender was meant to refer to those aspects of a role which are culturally determined, and sex to those which are biologically determined. Unfortunately, the distinction does not work. When we trace the use of gender and sex through various writings, and even through the writings of one author, it becomes obvious that gender and sex are used interchangeably. This suggests that the difficulty lies in the actual link between biological and social aspects of sex rather than in a lack of terms which describe the two aspects. The example of breastfeeding *v* bottlefeeding is a perfect example of how biological sex differences are linked to social factors.

'Sex roles' is the only widely used concept which combines a culturally determined behaviour pattern (roles) with a biological variable (sex). The only other remotely comparable concept is age roles. Here the difference is that age roles are not constant for one individual over time – if we live to a ripe old age we will have passed through all age roles – whereas one does not usually change one's sex. Age identifies stages in one's life, whereas sex is a more or less immutable criterion that remains stable over a lifetime. A direct parallel to sex roles would be race roles – and there is no such term, although there are different behaviour expectations and patterns for members of different races within the same society. The lack of the concept of race role indicates that we do not explain different behaviour patterns on the basis of race itself but rather in terms of a power differential which coincides with racial distinctions.

At the language level, the concept of sex roles is confusing. At the social level, analysis of sex roles (or gender roles) and sex identity (or gender identity) have a tendency to lead to reification. Sex roles refer to statistical distributions of behaviour patterns, and sex identity refers to statistical distributions of character attributes within given cultures. Both have therefore an element of variability. Since, however, their attribute – sex – is a constant for most people, there is a tendency to perceive what is a cultural variable as a cultural constant, an assumption that sex roles and sex identities are similar for all people of one sex. One of the topics that will be pursued in this book is the question whether it makes sense to try to identify universally applicable sex roles and sex identities.

We started out by observing the paradox of the antithetical tie of the criticism to the object of criticism (which, of course, is as applicable to this book as to any other). One of the ways in which this paradox is played out is at the level of language. Another way in which it manifests itself is in the way emphases are placed. Just as an atheist who continues to try to prove that God does not exist continues to emphasise the importance of God, so a scholar who continues to examine sex roles continues to emphasise and possibly overemphasise their importance. A sex role is not a sex role if we cannot demonstrate a constant difference in behaviour expectations on the basis of sex. Since sex roles are universally present (every society has them) and sex is a universal variable, and since we are only concerned with differences (where there is no sex difference, there is nothing to discuss), we tend to think that every important activity or trait is differentiated on the basis of sex. Nevertheless, there are many things we do in our lives which are shared by people of both sexes – we all eat, sleep, drink, play, rejoice, are ashamed, sad, envious, etc. But to the degree to which such activities are *not* differentiated by sex, they are ignored in this context.

This leads to a distortion of the differences over the similarities of the sexes. Once this trend towards exaggerating differences has started, it is difficult to come up with an explanation of observed sex differences — of which there are many, of course — in terms other than sex itself, simply *because* sex is seen to be of such overriding importance. This, of course, leads us back to exactly the biological fallacy of trying to explain social facts by biological facts which we initially set out to avoid. In order to find an explanation for a social sex difference we must introduce variables other than sex itself. In other words, both in terms of the language employed and in terms of explanations offered we must transcend sex rather than accept it as relevant if we wish to overcome sexism in language and thought.

There is yet another way in which the paradoxical antithetical tie of feminist thought to sexism shows itself, and that is in the area of practical-political concerns. Most feminists are committed to the abolition of sex roles. In other words, the only good sex difference tends to be an absent one. However, because we put the stress on sex differences rather than similarities, we tend not to notice the absence of sex differences where it occurs, and because our language is tied to sex, our vocabulary is not adequate to describe the absence of sex differences when it occurs. In terms of practical-political issues this leads to a dilemma.

As long as we distinguish all social differences in terms of sex we have no gauge which lets us determine which social sex differences should concern us as incidences of injustice and which should not. Suppose we had a society in which there was absolutely equal opportunity for females and males of all ages to go into all occupations. (Such a society does not, of course, exist anywhere.) Suppose further that we would find that in such a society the majority of women (but not all) would go into one set of occupations, and the majority of men (but not all) into another. Would this be a matter for concern? If the intent is to abolish sex roles, it would be, because statistically speaking we would find different behaviour patterns in terms of occupational choice on the basis of sex. Theoretically, if we wanted to abolish sex roles, we would then have to coerce women and men into jobs which neither of them wanted.

This is of course a far-fetched example, because at the present time there is very little true choice of occupation for anybody; in addition the female-dominated jobs tend to be more undesirable on a number of characteristics such as pay, prestige, autonomy, security, fringe benefits, etc. Nevertheless, the issue is a real one. Only if we have a criterion which is itself *not* tied to sex can we come up with equitable solutions for sexual inequality. The lack of such a criterion will necessarily result in mechanistic notions of equality and equal opportunity.

In this book, I have used the concept of the double standard as one such criterion which allows us to determine whether an identified sex difference is a matter for concern or not. A double standard implies that two things which are the same are measured or evaluated by different standards. Usually, the concept of the double standard is used in a strictly sexual sense, meaning that men have greater sexual freedom than women and boys than girls. This is, however, only the most dramatic expression of using two different measures to judge and evaluate the same behaviour. Since sex has implications for behaviour in an almost infinite range of areas, it is a useful concept for all types of behaviours in which sex plays a role. A good example can be found in the following verse, copied from a poster (source unknown).

A business man is aggressive;
    a business woman is pushy.
A business man is good on details;
    she's picky.
He loses his temper because he's so involved with his job;
    she's bitchy.
He follows through;
    she doesn't know when to quit.
He stands firm;
    she's hard.
His judgments are
    her prejudices.
He is a man of the world;
    she's been around.
He drinks because of the excess job pressure;
    she's a lush.
He isn't afraid to say what he thinks;
    she's mouthy.
He exercises authority diligently;
    she's power-mad.
He's close-mouthed;
    she's secretive.
He climbed the ladder of success;
    she's slept her way to the top.

16

He's a stern task master;
    she's hard to work for.

If we define as a double standard 'all norms, rules and practices which evaluate, reward and punish identical behaviour of women and men differentially' (Eichler, 1977, p. 14), we need to do two things in order to establish the presence of a double standard: we need to demonstrate that behaviour which is being evaluated or measured is in fact the same, and that different rewards and punishments ensue for the sexes. This is not necessarily as simple as might be thought at first glance. For one of the things that happens when a double standard is systematically applied is that identical behaviours are not defined as the same but as different due to the sex of the performer and the social context in which they take place.

This is so because there is always an element of interpretation present. Let us consider a non-sexual example. If one kills in the name of the state, one is either a hero (e.g. a brave soldier) or simply a good employee (e.g. an executioner, a policeman shooting and killing a suspect during duty). If one kills without permission of the state, one is a murderer. In both cases, some people end up dead. Nevertheless, the process of killing is measured by different standards, which is reflected in different languages. In one case, the process is called murder; in the other, execution or protection of your country.

Evaluation of behaviour, which is an aspect of the double standard, therefore plays a role. The prevailing interpretation of a particular action is challenged by a new look at the action itself. If a state considers the protection of private property as more important than the protection of individual lives, it will allow a home-owner who catches a burglar in the act of burglarising to kill the burglar. If the state considers individual life as more important, the home-owner who defends his or her property by taking somebody else's life will be charged with manslaughter.

The interpretation of the same act — shooting a burglar — depends on a superordinate value system. The same is true for all instances in which identical behaviours are interpreted and therefore rewarded and punished differentially. We can only charge that differentiating between different kinds of killing is an instance of a double standard if we believe that the killing of a human is illegitimate in all cases unless it be in a direct one-to-one self-defence which is not at issue here.

Showing that something which has been considered different is really the same therefore involves a questioning of who decides the legitimacy of various possible interpretations, i.e. the power structure that decides on rewards and punishments, and offering an alternative interpretation of the process.

When we turn to the double standard in the sexual sphere, and come to evaluations of, for example, non-marital sex in societies where this is interdicted for 'respectable' girls, we find that, although both a young man and a young woman have engaged in non-marital sex, it is considered 'normal' for the young man, but reprehensible for the young woman since she has now lost her honour. (Occasionally it can be recouped if the young man agrees to marry her.) And indeed, given the cultural evaluations which prevail in this type of society, the young woman *has* lost her honour while the young man has not. The consequences of the same behaviour — engaging in non-marital sex — are therefore certainly different.

When arguing that this is an example of a double standard, in which the same behaviour has been punished differentially on the basis of sex, we are therefore questioning the legitimacy of the culture to dispense different punishments on the basis of presently accepted sex roles. Instead, we argue that young men and young women should suffer equally — or not at all — for comparable actions.

This is a necessary step in all analyses of a double standard. One of the more important examples in this context is the issue of work. Until recently, work was equated with paid work only. Unpaid work was therefore considered non-work and, since only work deserved pay, not worthy of pay. In other words, an activity did not qualify for pay because it was unpaid. Recent analyses of the work women do has demonstrated that women do a lot of work which is substantially comparable to work done by men but women do it without pay. If we put the stress on the behaviours themselves — the work process — it is clear that a double standard has been applied which has differentially rewarded the sexes for engaging in identical behaviour — men are more likely to be paid for their work, women are more likely not to be paid. This, as in the case of the non-marital sexual relations, involves a reinterpretation of behaviours from the premise of looking only at the behaviours irrespective of the sex of the performer. Again, it challenges the legitimacy of a prevailing interpretation of the basis of the premise that essentially women and men should always be treated equally for equal behaviours.

In other words, in order to identify a double standard as a double standard in a society which adheres to this double standard we must have a critical attitude towards that society or else we will be unable to identify the double standard as such. This is so because power and knowledge are always intimately linked. The old adage that knowledge is power is certainly true, but the reverse, that power generates knowledge, is equally true. It is for this reason that knowledge about an underprivileged group, such as women, can only progress in small steps. A totally powerless group is totally mute. Protesting one's powerlessness is the first step towards gaining power. Only as a group finds a collective voice and collectively questions the legitimacy of an existing power structure can other data be generated which can then be used to challenge the validity of the viewpoint of the powerful group.

Feminist research over the past few years has produced a tremendous wealth of studies which challenge many of the assumptions held about women. This having been done, we can now start to criticise the knowledge-producing structures themselves, as well as the knowledge produced. This book concentrates on issues of the double standard in social science thinking, not by giving a comprehensive overview, but by picking up salient concepts and examples to examine them for manifestations of a thinking based on a double standard in interpreting the behaviour of the sexes. Such examination, if successful, should eventually lead to a different evaluation of behaviours.

I shall first be looking at some of the important literature on sex roles and arguing that the concept itself is premised on a double standard and is useful only as a descriptive variable but never as an explanatory variable. Sex identity, which represents the internalisation of sex roles at the individual level, holds the same difficulties. As an example I will examine Masculinity-Feminity scales and argue that they are based on a differential evaluation of identical character traits for people of different sexes, therefore on a double standard. I will then look critically at some of the literature which tries to overcome this problem, namely the literature on androgyny, and argue that it suffers from the same problem. Lastly, I will take a look at sex-change operations and argue that they are an extreme, but logical, outcome of a systematically applied double standard.

In the following chapter, I will look critically at various approaches to stratification, including class analysis, and argue that any definition of class as currently conceived is based on a differential evaluation of the same behaviours on the basis of sex, and that for that reason they constitute unacceptable classification systems. This does not invalidate the substantive questions raised by stratification theories, but it does suggest that we need an entirely new way of answering them. Finally, since knowledge and power are always connected, and our insights into the relations of the sexes will only change as the relationship itself changes, I will try to elaborate some principles of feminist scholarship, and discuss some of the current issues in the feminist movement which are of overriding political concern.

Note

1. The distinction of the three functions has profited from a discussion in my Advanced Research Seminar of Education, Women and Gender Relations, 1979, and especially from a presentation by Rona Achilles. The ideas were further developed by Nancy Sheldon, Susan Bazilli, Hanneke van Leeuwen and Martha Tenjo.

References

Eichler, Margrit, 'The Double Standard as an Indicator of Sex-Status Differentials', *Atlantis,* vol. 3 no. 1 (1977), pp.1-21.
Moulton, Janice, George M. Robinson, Cherin Elias, 'Sex Bias in Language Use. "Neutral" Pronouns that Aren't', *American Psychologist* (Nov. 1978), pp. 1032-6.
Wade, Nicholas, 'Bottle-Feeding: Adverse Effects of a Western Technology', *Science,* vol. 184, no. 4132 (5 April 1974), pp. 45-8.

2 THE DOUBLE STANDARD IN BEHAVIOUR EXPECTATIONS: THE INADEQUACY OF THE SEX ROLES APPROACH

In all societies, people have different ideas as to what constitutes proper behaviour for women and men. Girls and boys are socialised into their different roles. Socialisation into sex roles is based upon differentially rewarding boys and girls (and women and men) for identical behaviour, thus making them gradually prefer those behaviours which are considered 'sex appropriate' over those which are considered 'sex inappropriate'. In other words, sex role socialisation is the systematic teaching of a double standard, and it has been successful when the double standard has been internalised to such a degree that any of its manifestations seems just 'natural' to the people affected by it.

When we study sex roles, we study behaviour expectations as well as actual behaviours. Normally, researchers distinguish between 'persons studied and those not studied, i.e. between *subjects* and *nonsubjects.* A special category of persons who are nonsubjects is researchers conducting the study, the investigators' (Thomas and Biddle, 1966, p.24, their emphasis). A sociologist who studies the roles of certain types of people (e.g. doctors, cab drivers, parachute jumpers, etc.) has the option to be a nonsubject. However, the situation is fundamentally different for a person who studies sex roles. In all instances, he or she remains a male or female person to whom certain behaviour expectations are brought on the basis of his or her sex. In addition, information gathered from informants about sex roles is likely to be influenced by the sex of the informant(s) (e.g., Silverman, 1974). As far as sex roles are concerned, the sex of the investigator and of the informant must be seen as a definite factor in the interpretation of sex roles.

This is an important and often neglected problem in the study of sex roles. Another problem is the confusion of normative and actual behaviour. Let us assume that we come upon a group of mothers who abuse their children. In so far as there are no negative sanctions against such behaviour within this group of people, and in so far as it is a commonly expected type of behaviour, child abuse is part of an actual pattern of maternal behaviour, it is part of a sex role. However, the tendency within sociology would be to treat these mothers as 'unnatural mothers', since according to our own sex role stereotypes mothers are not only supposed not to abuse their children, but to love their children. 'Mothers love their children' — we consider 'motherlove' a statement of fact rather than a normative statement ('mothers should love their children'). In this hypothetical case, a normative prescription has been elevated to the level of actual behaviour, and the actual behaviour is misinterpreted as a deviation from some fictitious norm. As scientists we should, of course, note instead the discrepancy between actual behaviour and normative prescription and discuss the lack of fit between them.

We must, therefore, be careful not only to distinguish male from female perceptions of sex roles but also ideal from actual sex role behaviours. Rather than identifying and discussing 'a sex role', therefore, we must identify and discuss which of ten possible versions of a sex role we are talking about.

Ten Possible Versions of a Sex Role

 1. Male perception of actual female behaviour
 2. Male perception of ideal female behaviour
 3. Female perception of actual female behaviour
 4. Female perception of ideal female behaviour
 5. Actual female behaviour
 6. Female perception of actual male behaviour
 7. Female perception of ideal male behaviour
 8. Male perception of actual male behaviour
 9. Male perception of ideal male behaviour
10. Actual male behaviour

Actual female or male behaviour suggests that there is an 'objective' version of a sex role which is independent of male or female perceptions. In some instances this is not the case since it is impossible to separate the perception of a situation from the actual situation. Family power may be an example of this.[1] In other cases, however, we can determine actual behaviours with a fair degree of objectivity. For instance, filming a housewife's day would be a relatively objective way of assessing the tasks a housewife performs, and the pattern discovered would be likely to be different from what women think they do, from what they think they should do, and from what men think women do or should do.

Given the existence of at least two different versions of the same sex role, a great amount of confusion is possible. Three types of confusion, however, seem to predominate in the sex roles literature:

(a)   the equation of the ideal sex role with the actual sex role;
(b)   the ignoring of the female perception (with very few exceptions, this more or less eliminates versions 3, 4, 6 and 7); and
(c)   the equation of the male perception with male and female actual behaviours.

Let us, as an example, examine a passage from a recent overview of sex roles in primitive societies. All emphases are added.

An Example of the Overextension of the Male Perspective: Sex Roles and Social Sanctions

Sex Roles and Social Sanctions [Version 1]
Most of the *restrictions imposed by primitive societies upon a woman's freedom* stem from one or another aspect of her reproductive role. *Restrictions connected with pregnancy* have been noted, as well as those *imposed during the period after childbirth and during lactation.* Among many peoples, *limitations are placed upon the activities of women during their menstrual periods as well.* Societies vary markedly, however, in the degree to which they *curtail a menstruating woman's participation in social life.* In a few societies, the only *restriction placed upon her activities* is that she may not engage in sexual intercourse. In a few other societies, menstruation involves strict seclusion and isolation. The majority of primitive peoples *surround the woman with specific restrictions*, leaving her free to move about with certain exceptions. Always *she is forbidden sexual intercourse, frequently she may not go into the gardens, and may not participate in religious ceremonies.*

With respect to *restrictions imposed upon women during menstruation*, Stephens (1961) marshals considerable cross-cultural evidence linking the prevalence and intensity of menstrual taboos to various child-rearing practices. His conclusion is that those practices that tend to produce male castration anxiety are associated with *placing more severe restrictions on women during menstruation.* In a parallel cross-cultural study, Young and Bacadayan (sic) (1965) present evidence in support of a different hypothesis, namely that *menstrual taboos are institutionalized ways for men to discriminate against women* and that they are most severe in societies where male are dominant and tightly organized. Whatever the reason may be for *differential treatment of menstruating women*, it appears that where modern hygiene has been introduced the tendency is for the *restrictions to become minimal.* Menstrual taboos disappear except for the restriction on sexual activity, and the period of confinement after childbirth is abbreviated. It seems clear that *modern technology is making it possible to do away with some of the more stringent restrictions imposed upon women* that are associated with their *reproductive cycle. Even under optimum conditions*, however, *woman's reproductive role cannot but help interfere with many activities that men are relatively free to perform.* (Ford, 1970, pp.31-2)

This passage reads like a perfectly objective, univalent description of, as its title says, sex roles and social sanctions. When we look more closely at the passage, it turns out not to be a description but an implicit interpretation from a male perspective, all the more persuasive because it does not seem to be interpretative. Besides interpreting the meaning of sexual taboos in primitive societies the passage also offers a value judgement concerning the relative position of women in primitive and modern societies.

If we examine the passage, and particularly the italicised parts, we find that women are consistently treated as objects rather than as subjects. By simply considering the sentence structure we find that women are presented in the passive mode. For example, restrictions are imposed on them, limitations are placed on them, their participation is curtailed, they are surrounded with restrictions, they are forbidden, they may not do something, they are differentially treated. In only a few sentences is there a simple description of an activity or a custom, and in no case does the woman act as a subject.

Let us, for an example, rewrite the above passage in neutral, non-interpretative, non-judgemental, descriptive, 'objective' terms. It then reads as follows:

Sex Roles and Social Sanctions – Version 2
Most of the taboos concerning women in primitive societies are related to one or another aspect of woman's reproductive role. Pregnancy taboos have been noted as well as post-partum taboos and taboos concerning lactation. Among many peoples there are menstrual taboos, as well. Societies vary markedly, however, in the type of menstrual taboos that are prevalent. In a few societies, the only female taboo is one on sexual intercourse. In a few other societies, menstruation involves strict seclusion and isolation. The majority of primitive peoples have specific taboos for women, leaving them free to move about with certain exceptions. Always, there is a sexual

intercourse taboo; frequently, there is a gardening taboo (or a taboo against entering the garden), a cooking taboo or a taboo against touching the male's hunting or fishing gear, and a taboo on participation in religious ceremonies.

With respect to menstrual taboos, Stephens (1961) marshals considerable cross-cultural evidence linking the prevalence and intensity of menstrual taboos to various child-rearing practices. His conclusion is that those practices that tend to produce male castration anxiety are associated with more elaborate menstrual taboos. In a parallel cross-cultural study, Young and Bacadayan (sic) (1965) present evidence in support of a different hypothesis, namely that menstrual taboos are institutionalised ways for men to discriminate against women and that they are more severe in societies where males are dominant and tightly organised. [This sentence cannot be reformulated since the passive form was used explicitly rather than implicitly.] Whatever the reason may be for differences in menstrual taboos, it appears that where modern hygiene has been introduced the tendency is for the taboos to become greatly reduced in number (or to become much less elaborate). Menstrual taboos disappear except for the taboo on sexual activity, and the period of confinement after childbirth is abbreviated. It seems clear that modern technology is altering the taboos associated with the reproductive cycle of women. Under all conditions, however, the different reproductive roles of the sexes will invariably result in a different set of activities for the sexes.

Rewriting the passage in a neutral, non-judgemental manner allows us to entertain three possible interpretations of sexual taboos, to consider three different perspectives, namely that the taboos are imposed by men on women, or else that the taboos are imposed by women on men, since they always refer to a temporary change in a male-female relationship (e.g. if there is a cooking taboo during menstruation it not only means that a woman will not cook, but also that some man will not have his food cooked by this particular woman; and for every woman who observes a sexual intercourse taboo because of menstruation there is some man who cannot have sexual intercourse with this specific woman during the tabooed period, or, alternatively, a man is constantly in potential danger if a woman chooses to conceal from him that she is menstruating and starts to seduce him in order to do him wilful harm). Thirdly, the word 'imposed' may be altogether wrong, since it implies a conscious voluntary action, and sexual taboos may simply be interpreted as an *expression* of the power that women hold over men. As Stephens in another study that 'marshals considerable cross-cultural evidence' states: '... menstrual taboos are unusual in that they appear to reflect hardly any solicitude for the safety of the menstruating woman herself' (Stephens, 1962, p.95).

A number of societies have the belief that the menstruating woman can endanger the whole community by bringing supernatural punishment or by blighting the food supply. She may also be dangerous to special categories of persons, such as sick people. However, there were no reports of menstruating women being dangerous to other women (with the exception of individual females who fell into one of these special categories) ...

By far the dominant belief ... appears to be that menstruating women are dangerous to men. (Stephens, 1962, p.96)

Is it not a considerable degree of power if a woman, simply by violating a sexual taboo, can harm the entire male community (since menstruating women are not harmful to other women)? And if such great power inheres in female sexuality, is it not a form of voluntary restraint from harming men on the part of women if they observe the taboos related to their sexuality?

Who is to say, further, that women do not simply refuse to engage in certain tasks and activities during certain recurrent periods? It is only the invidious use of ostensively neutral labels which prevent us from recognising this possibility, such as Young and Bacdayan's attempt to construct different types of menstrual taboos, and in the process labelling three of them like this: 'menstruants *not allowed* to have contact with male things, especially such capital equipment as bows or fishing gear', 'menstruants *not allowed* to cook for men', 'menstruants *must* spend their menstrual period in menstrual huts' (Young and Bacdayan, 1967, p.96, emphases added).

Let us now rewrite the original passage by Ford once more, this time assuming that women are the active agents in the maintenance of sexual taboos. We then receive a very different image of sexual taboos.

Sex Roles and Social Sanctions – Version 3
Most of the female taboos in primitive societies are directly related to one or another aspect of woman's reproductive role. Pregnancy taboos have been noted as well as post-partum taboos and taboos concerning lactation. Among many peoples, women refrain from

certain activities during their menstrual periods as well. Societies vary markedly, however, in the degree to which the woman refuses to participate in social life during menstruation. In a few societies, the only activity she refuses to engage in is sexual intercourse. In a few other societies, menstruation may lead women to completely separate themselves, both physically and socially, from men. In the majority of primitive peoples, women engage only in specific withdrawals and maintain their usual social relations in all other cases. Always, however, the woman refuses to engage in sexual intercourse; frequently, she will not enter the gardens or refuses to cook for men. Her power may be such that, if she touches the man's hunting or fishing gear, calamity may befall him. She will only do so, therefore, if she wishes him ill. Finally, she may refuse to participate in certain religious ceremonies.

With respect to menstrual taboos, Stephens (1961) marshals considerable evidence linking the prevalence and intensity of menstrual taboos to various child-rearing practices. His conclusion is that those practices that tend to produce male castration anxiety are associated with more drastic refusals of women during menstruation to perform certain services and with higher imputed power of female sexuality to harm men. In a parallel cross-cultural study, Young and Bacadayan (sic) (1965) present evidence in support of a different hypothesis, namely that menstrual taboos are institutionalised ways for men to discriminate against women and that they are most severe in societies where males are dominant and tightly organised. Whatever the reason may be for different practices of menstruating women, it appears that where modern hygiene has been introduced the tendency is for the withdrawal of women to become minimal. Menstrual taboos disappear except for the refusal of sexual intercourse, and the period of physical withdrawal after childbirth is abbreviated. It seems clear that modern technology is making it impossible for women to practice their more drastic forms of physical withdrawal and refusal to engage in certain activities that used to be associated with their reproductive cycle. Even in the worst case, however, woman's reproductive role will still enable her to refuse participation in some male-dominated activities.

By now the third version may appear as fantastic, one hopes, as the first one appears. Which of them comes nearer to the truth cannot be determined at the present time. Certainly, however, the first version can no longer be accepted. The truth lies probably in a mixture of all three versions — in some societies sexual taboos for women may, indeed, be imposed on women by men, in others they may indicate an imposition of behaviour patterns on men on the part of women. In all cases, however, they must surely be seen as expressions of female power lodged in female sexuality. If, indeed, female sexual taboos become fewer in technologised societies, this would indicate a loss of power in female sexuality. Obviously, we can no longer assume that 'Surely the most obvious interpretation of menstrual taboos is that they are institutionalized ways in which males in primitive societies discriminate against females' (Young and Bacdayan, 1967, p.100). The only thing that seems sure, at the present time, is that the androcentric bias has been so prevalent in Western anthropology that it has blinded anthropologists from recognising expressions of female power as just that, instead interpreting them as expressions of female powerlessness (cf. Eichler, 1975).

This is, on the one hand, an indication of the overextension of the male perspective on the subject of sex roles in primitive societies. At the same time, it indicates the penetration of the double standard into purportedly objective analysis.[2] Equivalent social customs are interpreted differently depending on the sex of the subject of the investigation. It is a well-known fact that in many primitive societies royalty are surrounded with many restrictions, especially in their sexual activities. Among the Bemba, for example,

> The sex life of the chief has . . . a mysterious effect on the welfare of all his people. His sexual power gives vigour and 'warmth' to the land. Hence, the phrase *ukukafye calo* (to warm the land), and the rule that a territorial chief should never sleep with a woman when travelling outside his territory. By a sexual act the *mfumu* can bless seeds or other objects required for the use of the tribe.
>
> But this power is alike the cause of danger. By breaking a sex taboo — such as approaching the spirits without the right ceremony of purification, the ruler can bring incalculable harm on the community. (Human Relations Area Files, FQR Bemba, p.643)

We are obviously dealing with sexual taboos on the part of the chief here, and these same sexual taboos are seen as an indication of his inherent power. Why is the same type of power interpreted as subjection, degradation and inferiority on the part of women? Surely *not* because they are different in nature but only because the interpreter was so biased in his thought patterns that he could not perceive of the possibility of women being powerful. Indeed, there are cases reported in which women utilise their sexual status as means to achieve desired ends. Evans-Pritchard, for example, reports (but does not emphasise or interpret the meaning) that among the Azande a woman 'will often refuse to have intercourse with her husband, making the excuse that she is in her menstrual periods' (Evans-Pritchard, 1974, p.45). If she is honest, he continues, she will of course not do so, or else she will demonstrate the truth of her reason by showing her husband the blood on her thighs so that he will know that she is speaking the truth.

There are some anthropologists who have recognised the power that may inhere in female sexuality. Maranda (1974, pp.177-202), for example, has observed that among the Lau menstruation is seen as a joyful holiday from the daily duties of women. And Devereux, in a case study of genital bleeding among the Mohave Indians, concludes that

> it is erroneous to interpret the secluding of menstruating women as a sign of their temporary social degradation. On the contrary, these restrictions and special attitudes merely indicate that they are set apart from, and, in many ways, set above the rest of mankind. Their seclusion must therefore be thought of as essentially identical with the 'honorific' restrictions (etiquette, taboos) imposed upon rulers and other sacred persons which, superficially, appear to serve the exalted persons, but are actually meant to protect ordinary people from the overwhelming *mana* of kings. In fact, etiquette frequently restricts in an inconvenient and awkward manner the freedom and psychological spontaneity of these human reflections of 'divine' omnipotence. (Devereux, 1950, pp.252-3)

By considering the female perspective, we may therefore get a radically different picture of the meaning of social customs than the one provided by the male perspective.

In spite of the fact that there are discrepancies in the interpretation of specific sex roles there is unanimity about the universal existence of sex roles in all human societies. This seems to be one of the few unshakeable truths in this area of study. The universal *existence* of sex roles has led to a search for the universal *nature* of sex roles which would obtain in primitive as well as in complex societies. This search has led to the identification of several sex differences which are widely accepted as being of a universal or near-universal nature. Let us now examine these purportedly universal sex differences.

Purported Cross-cultural Regularities in Sex Differences

Mussen (1969) summarises well the prevailing notions with respect to the nature of sex role differences. We shall therefore use him as a convenient starting-point. According to Mussen:

> It is a banal truth that the individual's sex role is the most salient of his many social roles. No other social role directs more of his overt behaviour, emotional reactions, cognitive functioning, covert attitudes and general psychological and social adjustments. Linton observed that 'the division of the society's members into age-sex categories is perhaps the feature of greatest importance for establishing participation of the individual in culture' (Linton, 1945, p.63) . . .
>
> Although each culture has its own definitions of male and female roles and characteristics, there are some impressive cross-cultural regularities, some core concepts of masculinity and feminity (D'Andrade, 1966). For example, the majority of societies around the world organize their social institutions around males, and in most cultures men are more aggressive and dominating, have greater authority and are more deferred to than women. They are generally assigned the physically strenuous, dangerous tasks and those requiring long periods of travel. Women, on the other hand, generally carry out established routines, minstering to the needs of others, cooking, and carrying water. The husband-father role is *instrumental*, i.e. task-oriented and emotion-inhibited in nearly all cultures, and the wife-mother role is customarily more *expressive*, i.e. emotional, nurturant, and responsible (Parsons, 1955). (Mussen, 1969, pp.707-8, his emphasis)

Some of the postulated regularities do not require long discussion. The first postulate, that social institutions tend to be organised around males, is clearly wrong in one sense and possibly right in another. Surely the family is one of the most important institutions in the world, and who would wish to maintain that the family is built around males? But even in other major institutions in which the role of women is not so immediately visible, the postulate might rather read that we have tended to ignore the role of women in social institutions (cf. Kanter, 1975) than that the role of women is negligible. The role of women within social institutions is often different from the role of men, but neither religion, nor the economy, nor the legal system can be imagined to continue unchanged in *any* society if the females' roles within them were to be abolished. The only social institutions that are 'organised around males' are male secret societies and fraternities, and, of course, this needs to be counterbalanced by the fact that there are also female secret societies and sororities. On the other hand, if we take the statement to mean that the major social institutions are organised more for the benefit of men than for the benefit of women, it becomes a plausible statement, but one that needs to be empirically tested.

It is manifestly true that in most societies women do the cooking and carrying of water. Since these are specific rather than general designations of female activities we can simply accept them as true. There is also sufficient evidence that men tend, in general, to be more aggressive (in a physical sense) than women that it seems reasonable to accept this statement for the moment as true (cf. Maccoby and Jacklin, 1974, pp.227-47). This leaves us with three other postulates concerning purportedly impressive cross-cultural regularities in sex roles:

1. Men do the physically strenuous, dangerous, and ambulatory tasks, women do the repetitive, stationary tasks and minister to the needs of others.
2. The wife-mother role is expressive, the husband-father role is instrumental.
3. Men are dominant, women are dominated, men have greater authority and are deferred to, women are ruled and defer.

Let us consider each of the three postulates in turn.

1. *The Postulate of a Consistent Division of Labour by Sex*

It is customary for social scientists to refer to Murdock's data on the division of labour by sex when attempting to prove that men do the physically strenuous, dangerous tasks and those requiring long periods of travel while women minister to the needs of others and carry out the established routines. Murdock himself postulates this (Murdock, 1965, pp.7-8). Therefore, we shall utilise Murdock's data to demonstrate that this postulate is not correct for primitive societies.

Table 2.1 is based on 224 tribes from all over the world. The first column gives the number of tribes in which the particular activity is confined exclusively to males. The second lists those in which women engage in the occupation only relatively infrequently or in a subordinate capacity. The third column enumerates the tribes in which the occupation is either carried on indifferently by both sexes or cooperatively by both. The fourth and fifth list the tribes in which the activity

Table 2.1: Comparative Data on the Division of Labour by Sex

	M	M−	−	F−	F	Per Cent
Metal working	78	0	0	0	0	100.0
Weapon making	121	1	0	0	0	99.8
Pursuit of sea mammals	34	1	0	0	0	99.3
Hunting	166	13	0	0	0	98.2
Manufacture of musical instruments	45	2	0	0	1	96.9
Boat building	91	4	4	0	1	96.0
Mining and quarrying	35	1	1	0	1	95.4
Work in wood and bark	113	9	5	1	1	95.0
Work in stone	68	3	2	0	2	95.0
Trapping or catching of small animals	128	13	4	1	2	94.9
Work in bone, horn and shell	67	4	3	0	3	93.0
Lumbering	104	4	3	1	6	92.2
Fishing	98	34	19	3	4	85.6
Manufacture of ceremonial objects	37	1	13	0	1	85.1
Herding	38	8	4	0	5	83.6
House building	86	32	25	3	14	77.0
Clearing of land for agriculture	73	22	17	5	13	76.3
Net making	44	6	4	2	11	74.1
Trade	51	28	20	8	7	73.7
Dairy Operations	17	4	3	1	13	57.1
Manufacture of ornaments	24	3	40	6	18	52.5
Agriculture − soil preparation and planting	31	23	33	20	37	48.4
Manufacture of leather products	29	3	9	3	32	48.0
Body mutilation, e.g., tattooing	16	14	44	22	20	46.6
Erection and dismantling of shelter	14	2	5	6	22	39.8
Hide preparation	31	2	4	4	49	39.4
Tending of fowls and small animals	21	4	8	1	39	38.7
Agriculture − crop tending and harvesting	10	15	35	39	44	33.9
Gathering of shellfish	9	4	8	7	25	33.5
Manufacture of non-textile fabrics	14	0	9	2	32	33.3
Fire making and tending	18	6	25	22	62	30.5
Burden bearing	12	6	33	20	57	29.9
Preparation of drinks and narcotics	20	1	13	8	57	29.5
Manufacture of thread and cordage	23	2	11	10	73	27.3
Basket making	25	3	10	6	82	24.4
Mat making	16	2	6	4	61	24.2
Weaving	19	2	2	6	67	23.9
Gathering of fruits, berries and nuts	12	3	15	13	63	23.6
Fuel gathering	22	1	10	19	89	23.0
Pottery making	13	2	6	8	77	18.4
Preservation of meat and fish	8	2	10	14	74	16.7
Manufacture and repair of clothing	12	3	8	9	95	16.1
Gathering of herbs, roots and seeds	8	1	11	7	74	15.8
Cooking	5	1	9	28	158	8.6
Water carrying	7	0	5	7	119	8.2
Grain grinding	2	4	5	13	114	7.8

Source: George P. Murdock, 'Comparative Data on the Division of Labour by Sex', *Social Forces* (October 1936 − May 1937), vol. 15, no. 4, p. 552.

is, respectively, predominantly and exclusively feminine. The percentages in the sixth column were obtained by scoring tribes in the first five columns 100, 75, 50, 25 and 0 per cent respectively and striking the average. It is thus a rough index of the degree of masculinity of an occupation in general (Murdock, 1936-7, pp.551-3).

At first glance, there seems to be some support for Mussen's statement, since, according to Murdock's data, the pursuit of sea mammals, hunting, and the trapping or catching of small animals are predominantly male activities which might be construed to require long periods of travel, and which may also be assumed to be dangerous. Further, mining and quarrying, work in stone, and lumbering — likewise predominantly male occupations — are customarily regarded as physically strenuous. However, grain grinding, which is often done by pounding or rubbing one stone on another, is certainly at least as strenuous and physically demanding as hunting — if not more so — and so are water carrying, and burden bearing, all of which are predominantly female occupations. Burden bearing is an interesting occupation for another reason. What burdens are there to carry in primitive societies? In nomadic tribes it might be tents, in most societies it might be fuel, and in all societies in which hunting is a major source of nutrition carrying the game would constitute a significant burden. Therefore, if women predominantly carry the burdens, it follows that they must be as physically mobile as their menfolk in order to be at hand when there are burdens to carry. We therefore find no substance to the generalisation that men are usually assigned the physically strenuous tasks that require long periods of travel. Whether or not the male tasks are more dangerous is more difficult to judge since there are different types of dangers (in modern societies, for instance, most accidents happen within the household and not within the quarries or factories)[3] and without the evidence of some statistics on injuries or death-rates by type of occupation we can make no judgement about the relative danger of any one occupation.

Let us now look at the female tasks. Women 'generally carry out the established routines, ministering to the needs of others'. Men, by implication, do not carry out established routines, and do not minister to the needs of others. When we reformulate Mussen's statement thus it is surprising. Why, for instance, should we regard metal working, weapon making, or the pursuit of sea mammals as less routine than gathering fruits, berries and nuts, gathering shellfish, gathering fuel or herbs, roots, and seeds? Supposedly, men do not minister to the needs of others. What then do we call it when men hunt game for an entire compound? If people other than the hunters partake of the meat or fish that has been caught, then, obviously, we must interpret the activity that led to the sharing of food as one way of ministering to a very basic need of all humans, namely providing food.

As far as the division of labour in primitive societies is concerned, there is no support for the notion of a consistent division of labour in terms of the nature of the tasks performed which, according to Mussen (and many others) show such marked regularity.

The situation in complex societies is somewhat more difficult to evaluate, since there is no comparable standard reference with respect to the division of labour by sex. When we disregard for a moment the basic division of labour between paid labour and unpaid housework, i.e. compare women in the labour force with men in the labour force, and when we take a broad time perspective, we find that at different times and in different countries women perform or have performed the most physically strenuous work that is performed or has been performed by men. Especially in the nineteenth century, both women and men used to work under gruesome conditions. Let us consider two examples of typically feminine occupations in nineteenth-century Britain: the textile worker and the dressmaker.

The following sections provide a graphic description of the dangers accompanying both occupations:

Concerning the health of mill women there was great divergence of opinion. One group contended that excessive labour where the temp-erature ranged from 84 to 90 degrees in the cotton-spinning depart-ment, and to 120 and 140 degrees in the linen mills, where the air was vitiated by the fluff in the carding-room and dust in the picking-room of cotton mills, and the workers wet to the waist, in the wet-spinning process of flax, stood in bare feet on the wet floor in a steamy atmosphere, was a menace to health. Poor ventilation was common. The older mills had too few windows. Those of the im-proved mills were often kept closed. In the usual airless work-room the smell of oil and gases further vitiated the atmosphere. The noise of machinery, which modern ingenuity had not yet conquered, added to the discomfort. All of the work was done standing, and piecers, according to the calculations given by Lord Ashley to Parlia-ment, travelled from seventeen to twenty-seven miles, with the addi-tional strain of turning the body round to the reverse direction four or five thousand times in a day. Meal-times before 1844 and later were often crowded out by the practice of cleaning the machinery at noon or by a rush of extra work. Food standing in the work-room and covered with fluff was eaten hurriedly, the workers often snatching a bit of it when they could. There were no proper rooms for dressing, or eating. Toilet facilities were inadequate. In many departments women worked where they had no protection from machinery, and their long hair and loose aprons exposed them more than the men. One girl who was caught by the clothes in a shaft revolving at great speed was given one hundred pounds damages when ten shillings would have paid for the enclosing of the machinery. Women were scalped, arms and fingers were crushed, and legs were wounded by unboxed machinery. . . Headaches, excessive fatigue, relaxed muscles, loss of appetite they traced to the long hours of tedious labour in a foul, hot atmosphere, and to lack of sleep from night work; and fallen arches, pains in the feet, the turned-in ankles and knees, the swelled legs, the enlarged veins, and the general weakness were attributed to continuous standing. Bad eyesight was an evil of many kinds of factory work; wounds and ulcers of the legs, of course. Certain diseases were attributed directly to mill work, such as asthma, chronic hoarseness, and consumption, brought on by breathing air choked with dust and fluff. Scrofula was also a frequent disorder. The workers were described as short and stunted in growth. (Neff, 1966, pp.37-59)

At the time, there was a group of defenders of the health of factory women one of whom went even so far as to show the healthful effects of working in 140′ degrees (ibid.). Depending on whom one reads, working in textile mills is pictured as a veritable hell or as a delectable heaven. However, the above description speaks for itself. Nor were the dressmakers any better off.

The long hours in a stifling atmosphere, with irregular meals of poor quality, insufficient rest, and no exercise, naturally broke down the health of even the strongest country girls. The factory report of 1834 had already given the opinion that the health of milliners was more affected by their work than that of factory girls. A physician quoted by Mr Grainger said: 'No men work so continuously with so little rest.' An indignant article in *Fraser's* stated that the seamstresses in London could hardly use their feet, and that spinal curvatures were common. . . Exhausted girls fainted. A constant supply of fresh hands from the country replaced the girls who were no longer of any use. Consumption and poor eyes, another witness stated, were the most common results of the violation of all rules of health. (Neff, 1966, pp.122-3)

Who would wish to maintain that such work was not dangerous, physically strenuous, and ambulatory? (The women had to get to their place of work just as the men had to.) In recent times, protective labour legislation has reserved some of the more physically strenuous jobs for men in some countries. It has been argued that this is not to the benefit of women, since these jobs are also usually more highly paid. A better strategy would be to remove working hazards, where avoidable, for both women and men, and otherwise to leave a free choice among physically strenuous jobs for those people who wish to accept them.

What about war as the extreme manifestation of physically dangerous work? It is certainly true that in most countries today women do not serve in the combat forces. However, the argument that therefore women are exempt from the greater risks of war is no longer applicable, and has not been applicable since the Second World War, and has been even less so in more recent years. The approximate number of mobilised persons who were killed or died of their wounds in the Second World War is 16,766,000, the estimated number of civilians who were killed or died from their injuries is 32,899,000 (Wood, 1968, p.26) – in other words, about double the number of civilians were killed than of those who had been mobilised. The modern weapons are non-discriminatory. Bombs kill everyone in their range, not just men. If biological or gas warfare is utilised, everybody within an affected area will die, not just the men. With some of the modern weapons, people on combat duty may actually be safer than civilians, if they have access to transportation and can escape certain types of assaults. Urban guerrillas and terrorists likewise attack people of both sexes and all ages. If war is not on one's own territory (e.g. if combat forces are sent into a foreign country) it is true that mobilised people incur a differentially higher risk of death or injury than those who are not mobilised. However, if we compare the proportion of people killed or injured in traffic accidents with the proportion of people killed or injured in recent wars we find that traffic constitutes a proportionally greater threat to our health and life than a war on somebody else's territory.[4]

As far as women in the labour force are concerned, Mussen's generalisation that men perform the dangerous, physically strenuous tasks cannot be accepted.

What about housework? The three major functions of housework are housekeeping (including cooking), childcare, and personal service to husbands, children and other people. Care of small children is extremely demanding physically as anybody will testify who has ever attempted to do it unaided. The most physically tiring aspect of childcare is lack of sleep — as long as a child needs night feedings or wakes frequently at night the mother is unlikely ever to catch up on her sleep and is likely to go through her days in a sort of daze. However, this applies only for as long as a child is quite young, and we are therefore talking only about a limited number of years since fertility has been drastically reduced in industrialised countries and is still on the decline. On the other hand, full-time housewives tend to have more children than women in the labour force, at least in Canada (Boyd, Eichler and Hofley, 1976, pp.42-3), and are therefore exposed to lack of sleep for a longer period of time. Over all, housekeeping has probably become considerably less physically demanding than it was some decades ago, but psychically more draining. A recent study found that Canadian housewives are more likely to commit suicide than married women in the labour force (Cumming, Lazer and Chisholm, 1975), suggesting that the position of 'housewife' has its own peculiar dangers.[5]

What about male ambulatory and female stationary work? First, I would suspect that the travel range and frequency of most men has been vastly overestimated. Most men are *not* executives who travel around the world on an expense account, or scientists who go frequently to conventions all over the world (and for that matter, most executives and scientists probably don't either). Most people in the labour force, male and female, alternate between their home and their place of work on a normal working day.

In as far as women are in the labour force, there is no reason to believe that they are less ambulatory than men; quite the contrary, they are likely to be more ambulatory since, in addition to participating in the labour force, they are also likely to do the shopping and the ferrying around of kids.

A recent time budget study has found that men engage in approximately four hours' more 'necessary travel' per week than women; however, when we add on to the category 'necessary travel' 'regular shopping' and 'visiting', both of which can be normally assumed to involve physical movement, the women in one-job couples spend more time on these three activities than the men in one-job couples.[6] Although this does not allow us to make any inference about the range of travel, it indicates that women spend more time moving about than do men, and specifically housewives more than men in the labour force.

The question of the ambulatory/stationary dichotomy is particularly interesting since it is simply a different formulation of the inside/ outside dichotomy which can be traced back to the ancient Egyptians and Greeks (Sullerot, 1972, pp.28-32). According to this notion, the woman belongs in the house, the man in the world. There are examples of cultures in which women are, indeed, largely restricted to their homes, most drastically perhaps in the institution of purdah (seclusion of women), and less dramatically in the form of the Victorian lady who is not supposed to venture into 'the world' without a male escort. However, does this justify us in claiming that women in general, all women, are less ambulatory than men, all men? At all times, including the Victorian age and including countries which observe purdah, there have always been servant women and women in other occupations who have been mobile. Keeping women in purdah 'is to some extent a "luxury" ' (Papanek, 1971, p. 522), and most men cannot afford it. The inside/ outside dichotomy (or the ambulatory/stationary dichotomy) therefore must be understood as an ideal for women, the male (and possibly also female) perception of the ideal female behaviour, rather than as actual female behaviour. When burying the ghost of ladylike behaviour we should make an effort to bury the inside/outside dichotomy as a description of reality at the same time.

As far as the repetitiveness of work is concerned, housework is certainly quite repetitious. So is, nowadays, the work of most people in the labour force. Indeed, housewives have a greater degree of autonomy in determining when to perform their repetitive tasks than most men in the labour force, with the exception of the small minority of professionals and executives.

What about ministering to the needs of others? There seems to be no doubt that women tend to look after more sick members of the family than men and that women are more heavily involved in child raising than men. This type of personal service has clearly been delegated to and accepted by many women and is appropriately described as nurturant behaviour or ministering to the needs of others. Indeed, childcare has apparently taken on more importance than it had previously. Reduced fertility and reduced infant mortality have encouraged women to make a greater emotional investment in each child. For example, at the beginning of this century infant mortality and fertility declined sharply for British factory women. Nevertheless, a large minority of women in factory cities still lost a child. Whereas previously this had been accepted matter-of-factly, under the changed circumstances this was no longer the case. The death of an infant now caused serious distress to the mother (cf. Stearns, 1973, esp. p.109). We can assume that the tendency to invest emotionally in each child has grown considerably since that time, and that this process has been repeated in all highly industrialised countries with low infant mortality rates.

Above, we have argued that hunting game should count as 'ministering to the needs of others' in primitive societies. Correspondingly, contemporary sociology maintains that the husband-father-breadwinner is ministering to the needs of his family by 'winning the bread'. I would suggest, however, that there is a crucial difference between providing game and earning money on behalf of the family. Primitive peoples live in a subsistence economy; when food is insufficient, the populace will go hungry. In modern complex states with a welfare orientation this is not the case — a family will survive, not comfortably, but nevertheless survive, even if no 'bread is won' by the husband-father. And since most people in industrialised countries are not living at a subsistence level, increased earnings of the husband-father-breadwinner are utilised to improve 'the quality of the life style'. This may or may not mean that a man ministers to the need of others when he tries to further his career as much as possible, irrespective of the fact that a man may rationalise his occupational behaviour in terms of the well-being of his family.

A most interesting study illustrates that relatively higher wages do not necessarily benefit all family members equally. In British working-class families in the Victorian age women usually received a fixed allowance out of the husband's salary for running the household. When male earnings rose above the subsistence level to comparative affluence (i.e. to 21 to 40 shillings a week) the position of the proletarian wife worsened, since the husband kept the larger share of the increase for himself. 'What seemed to be happening was that as wages advanced men took the bulk of the gain for themselves and abandoned the traditional pattern of turning most of their income over to their wives for family use' (Stearns, 1973, p.116). The reallocation of resources was reflected in a more rapid increase of male consumption items, particularly on food items such as meat and on recreation, whereas female consumption interests, primarily clothing and housing, lagged behind. The common pattern among workers with earnings above subsistence was to give a fixed allowance to their wife which did not proportionally increase with his increased earnings. Wives no longer knew how much their husbands earned and their economic role in the family declined (Stearns, 1973, p.117).

This is an important example because it illustrates that we cannot automatically identify the benefits which accrue to one family member with the over-all well-being of the family. Yet this is precisely what modern sociology tends to do — the breadwinning function of the husband-father is equated with his parental and spousal role and it is assumed that he is a better husband-father if he improves his job performance. However, in practice this equation does not necessarily hold after the basic necessities have been met.

The division of labour such that women concentrate on ministering to the needs of immediate family members is therefore more descriptive of industrialised complex societies than of primitive societies. Overall, there is no basis to the claim that we find cross-cultural consistency in any aspect of the division of labour by sex, besides the fact that, in some way, labour is divided by sex and that those occupations which require most physical aggression (such as combat forces) are predominantly male occupations.

2. *The Postulate of a Consistent Expressive/Instrumental Role Differentiation between Spouses*

In spite of the fact that there has been much recent criticism[7] of Parsons' instrumental/expressive dichotomy as applied to spouses, there is still a strong belief that the husband-father role is instrumental while the wife-mother role is expressive, not only in our own culture, but cross-culturally, as also implied by Mussen.

In order to understand the conceptual pair it is instructive to go back to the original formulation of the expressive/instrumental hypothesis. The instrumental/expressive dichotomy is partially co-terminous with an 'external'/'internal' dichotomy, and thus brings us back to the old 'inside'/'outside' dichotomy as discussed above.

> The area of instrumental function concerns relations of the system to its situation outside the system, to meet the adaptive conditions of its maintenance and equilibrium, and instrumentally establishing the desired relations to external goal-objects. The expressive area concerns the internal affairs of the system, and the maintenance of integrative relations between the members, and regulation of the patterns and tension levels of its component units. (Parsons, 1955, p.47).

There is nothing intrinsic in the conceptual pair which necessitates a juxtaposition, a mutual exclusivity of the two orientations. On the contrary, 'The instrumental complex and the complex of direct gratifications or expressions are both aspects of the total allocative mechanism of a concrete social system' (Parsons, Shils, and Olds, 1951, p.214). In terms of 'the total economy of the personality' 'adequate motivation of instrumental activities becomes impossible if the performance of instrumental roles imposes too heavy a sacrifice on the larger gratification interests of the personality' (Parsons, Shils and Olds, 1951, p. 215).

The instrumental/expressive dichtomy was first developed as a set of invariant problems of all role occupants, namely (1) problems of instrumental interaction, (2) problems of expressive interaction, and (3) integrative problems. As such, the discussion was, in the beginning, non-sex-specific and meant to be universally applicable. The designation of husband-father and wife-mother roles in terms of differential emphases was a later development. The distinction of instrumental and expressive leaders within the family emerged because the family was conceptualised as a small group. Bales had observed a differentiation of tasks between instrumental and expressive leaders in small groups of male undergraduate students, and the task differentiation there found was then applied to the family (Bales and Slater, 1955). This, of course, is highly questionable, because (a) cross-sex relations are typically not the same as same-sex relations, and (b) because it ignores the problem of permanence. If, indeed, a role differentiation develops with respect to specific tasks along the expressive/instrumental dimensions, this tell us nothing about the permanence of such differentiation. It is entirely possible that with different tasks and situations the prevailing role differentiation shifts to different actors.

The issue at stake, then, is not a direct criticism of the concepts themselves, but rather whether or not it is appropriate to designate the wife-mother as the expressive leader and the husband-father as the instrumental leader (Zelditch, Jr, 1955, pp.308-15) of the family. When the dichotomy was first introduced into the family literature, clearly the authors perceived of it as a matter of degree, not as the stark opposition that it later on assumed.

> ... though the general functions of this collectivity [the marriage relationship] in the superordinate systems are expressive, the *more* instrumental role in the subsystem is taken by the husband, the *more* expressive one by the wife. This is to say that externally, the husband has the primary adaptive responsibilities, relative to the outside situation, and that internally he is in the first instance 'giver-of-care', or pleasure, and secondarily the giver of love, whereas the wife is primarily the giver of love and secondarily the giver of care or pleasure. The husband role, that is, is prototypically closer to the 'mother' role, that of the wife, to the 'child' role. But both are

'mother' and 'child' to each other. (Parsons, 1955, p.151)

I wish to suggest that the designation of the mother-wife as expressive leader of the family and the designation of the husband-father as instrumental leader of the family stem from two related misperceptions: first, the exclusion of housework from the division of labour in society by misperceiving it as lying, somehow, outside the societal system of division of labour, and second, the construction of ego only as a male, never as a female, with alter being either a woman or a man. Both misperceptions are outgrowths of a basically androcentric view of society.

Let us first consider the exclusion of housework from the basic divisions of labour. The authors identify four fundamental problems in the instrumental system.

> The first derives from the fact that, *given the division of labour*, one or more alters must be the *beneficiaries* of ego's activities. In the terminology of economics, they must be the consumer of his product. ... Thus, the problem of disposal is the first problem of instrumental interaction. (Parsons, Shils and Olds, 1951, p.210) (first emphasis added)

If we include housework into the societal system of division of labour, clearly there are beneficiaries of the housewife's activities: her husband, children and other potential household members. The other family members consume the housewife's products of labour, her product is thus disposed.

> Secondly, insofar as ego specialized in a particular type of instrumentally significant activity, he becomes dependent on the output of one or more alters for meeting his own needs. ... there is an exchange problem here, too, growing out of the functional need, as it may be called, for ego to receive *remuneration* for his activities. Thus, the problem of remuneration is the second problem of instrumental interaction. (Parsons, Shils and Olds, 1951, p.210)

This, of course, is the crux of the problem. The housewife is *not* directly financially remunerated. However, the labour performed and the product produced are being remunerated financially if they are performed by anybody but a housewife — housekeepers, babysitters, specialised service agencies. Further, if we understand remuneration to mean *something* received in exchange rather than money received in exchange – and this seems entirely in line with the Parsonian interpretation since Zelditch (1955) applies the instrumental/expressive dichotomy to non-money societies – then, of course, the housewife does receive a remuneration in exchange for her products, even if it is a minimal remuneration, namely shelter, food and certain basic necessities such as clothing. Many of these are even legally embedded in societal structures – such as the legal right of the housewife to be supported by her husband. We can therefore conclude that the housewife does receive an – albeit small – remuneration for her products.

> Third, only in a limiting case will all the facilities that ego needs to perform his instrumental functions be spontaneously available to him. It will be necessary for him to acquire or secure access to some of them through arrangement with one or more alters, involving still a third set of exchange relations and the associated standard incorporated into the terms of exchange. This third instrumental problem is that of access to facilities. (Parsons, Shils, and Olds, 1951, p.210)

The need to arrange access to facilities is clearly the case in many functions related to housework: e.g. access to laundromats is necessary for those households without washing machines, and housewives negotiate for services with telephone installers, plumbers, interior decorators, repairmen for house-repairs as well as the repairs of general household implements, etc. However, all of these are relatively rare occurrences. Cooking, on the other hand, is a daily occurrence, and all urban housewives are to a very high degree dependent on an extremely complex system of food growth, preparation and distribution. A simple bottle of Ketchup has gone through a tremendously complex process before any housewife can put it on the table. As any imagined or real shortage of a particular product, due to a strike, failure in transportation, etc. demonstrates, urban centres are thrown into confusion when this complex chain of interaction is interrupted at any one of its links. Urban housewives cannot any longer substitute home-grown foods to replace those that are not available to them on the market. Therefore, the housewife is every bit as dependent upon a set of exchanges which allow access to facilities as is any other worker.

> Fourth, the product may not be capable of production by ego through his own unaided efforts. In this case he is dependent on still a fourth set of alters for collaboration in the joint instrumental pro-

cess. The process requires organization in which ego and alters coll-
aborate to produce a unitary result which is the object of instrumental significance. Thus, the fourth instrumental problem is the
problem of cooperation or collaboration. (Parsons, Shils and Olds,
1951, pp.210-11)

If we consider the socialisation of children into future independent,
self-sustaining, socially useful adult citizens as an instrumental function, then we see that the parents, and mothers in particular, need to
cooperate with other educators — school teachers, scout group leaders,
etc. — in the attempt to produce a person whose skills will be market-
able later on. If it is argued that the socialisation of children is essentially an expressive task, then we would also have to see the work of
all other educators, teachers at every level, as essentially expressive.
This, anybody would be unlikely to argue. Again, the primary difference in the function that is performed by the parents, and especially
the mother, is that she is not paid for her labour, while the other educators are.

It is, therefore, entirely possible to interpret housework/mothering
as instrumental action in terms of the instrumental system as set forth
by Parsons and his collaborators.

What about the expressive dimension? Clearly it inheres, too, in the
wife-mother roles, as it does in the husband-father roles. If we take seriously Bernard's dictum that marriage is not the same for both partners, that we have, in fact, 'his' marriage and 'her' marriage, (Bernard,
1972), then the misinterpretation of the wife-mother role as predominantly expressive becomes suddenly clear. The wife-mother role, is,
indeed, expressive in its functions if ego is the husband-father and the
wife-mother is simply his reference individual, whereas, above, we have
taken ego (the actor) to be the wife-mother and have implicitly treated
the husband-father and the child(ren) as the reference individuals.

The best description of the expressive, immediately adaptive, grati-
fying functions of the urban housewife for the husband-father is probably contained in Slater (1970, pp.73-4):

Having created a technological and social-structural juggernaut by
which they are daily buffeted, men tend to use their wives as opiates
to soften the impact of the forces they have set into motion against
themselves. Consider, for example, the suburban living pattern: husbands go to the city and participate in the twentieth century, while
their wives are assigned the hopeless task of trying to act out a rather

pathetic bucolic fantasy oriented toward the nineteenth. Men in their jobs must accept change — even welcome it and foster it — however threatening and disruptive it may seem. They do not know how to abstain from colluding daily in their own obsolescence, and they are frightened. Such men tend to make of their wives an island of stability in a sea of change. The wife becomes a kind of memento, like the bit of earth the immigrant brings from the old country and puts under his bed. He subtly encourages her to espouse absurdly old-fashioned views which he then ridicules when he is with his male associates. There is a special tone of good-natured condescension with which married men gather together to discuss the conservatism of their wives, and one senses how elegantly their ambivalence has been apportioned between them ('it's a great opportunity for me but of course the wife doesn't like to move — she has a lot of ties in the community, and of course the children in school and all . . . '). It permits the husband to be far more adaptable and amenable to change than he really feels.

The identification of the expressivity or instrumentality from the point of view of the male actors is, truly, the ultimate conception of women as 'the other sex' (de Beauvoir, 1952). If we accept the bread-winner-housewife urban family which obviously underlies Parsons' *et al.* conception of the allocation of expressive and instrumental leader-ship (although by now far less than half of all North American families fit this image, due to the prevalence of wives in the labour force and single-headed families) then we have, indeed, a situation in which, when the husband-father leaves for work, the wife-mother stays at home, remains behind, remains 'there'. Hence also the notion of housewifery as a stationary, housebound, non-ambulatory occupation — men do not see the women move around, be mobile, because when they return home the wife-mother is again 'there' to greet them — but do they know what she has done in between those two points of time, and if they know, is it relevant to their experience of the situation? For the man, she is *still* there; as far as she herself is concerned, she is *again* there, she, also, has returned. Since the interruptions of her presence from home go by and large unnoticed, since unobserved, they can be ignored, and for the husband the wife may symbolise, indeed, the stability of the system.

. . . while the husband-father is away at work or in the fields, the mother very often stays at home symbolizing the integrative focus of the system (even though her activities may be primarily instrumental during this phase of family activity). (Zelditch, Jr, 1955, p.312)

If we conceptualise ego as the wife-mother, as has been done implicitly above, then her activities become as instrumental for herself as those of the husband are instrumental in his own perception. The husband is, to the wife, certainly a source of immediate gratification or irritation, depending on positive or negative affective interplay between the spouses. He may therefore just as well symbolise to her the 'stability of the system' as she symbolises the stability of the system for him: by his regular return home, by his household help (however insignificant in volume it may be), by her feeling of 'doing it for him', and by his appreciation of the work done or at least by his unwavering expectation that it be done.

While it may, therefore, be profitable to explore the expressive and instrumental dimensions of both husband's and wife's activities, we cannot accept the bald statement (as, for example, formulated by Mussen, but also by many others, including Parsons himself) that the wife-mother role is expressive, and the husband-father role is instrumental. There is still another angle to this.

When we talk about the wife-mother role, we should, really, be talking about wife-mother-housekeeper roles, and when we talk about the husband-father role, we should, instead, be talking about the husband-father-breadwinner roles (where appropriate). Neglecting to do so has interesting repercussions. In the case of the woman, the instrumental housekeeping role is neglected probably because the man encounters the woman primarily in her wife-mother roles, the housekeeping is done while he is out of the house. In the case of the man the breadwinner role is seen of such overriding importance for the man that the husband-father roles of the man are defined in terms of his breadwinning role. If we look at the expressive/instrumental content of each of these roles separately, we find that the housekeeper and breadwinner roles are essentially instrumental roles, the wife and husband roles are primarily expressive, and the mother and father roles are both expressive and instrumental. If, as has been the case, the man's family roles are defined in instrumental terms only, we have substituted economic functions for emotional functions and have, to the degree that we have done so, dehumanised men. It is only very recently that some social scientists have started to see the equation of economic roles with emotional roles as a form of deprivation for men (cf. the collection of articles contained in Pleck and Sawyer, 1974). The incipient men's liberation movement is focusing, very appropriately, on the bringing back of emotionality into men's roles. Breadwinning can no longer be utilised as a rationalisation for the shirking of the husband-father family roles.

3. *The Postulate of Consistent Female Deference and Male Dominance*

In Chapter 3 we shall consider the theoretical utility of prevailing models of sex stratification. Here, we are only concerned with the factual correctness of the statement that in most cultures men are more deferred to than women and have greater authority than women.

There is an implicit assumption that deference behaviour indicates inferiority or subordination on the part of the deferring party, or authority on the part of the deferred to party. I would suggest that deference can in no way be regarded as an unambiguous, uni-dimensional phenomenon. On the one hand, people of superior status and great power are often deferred to, on the other hand, the Victorian lady, for instance, was also greatly deferred to yet certainly not dominant nor the carrier of authority. Deference, when it involves etiquette, can also be a means of restraining a person. If you have to wait until somebody opens the door for you in order to be able to walk through, it means that you are dependent on another person in your movements. The meaning of deference cannot, therefore, be seen as unambiguous and deferring behaviour should not be interpreted as a sure sign of subordination.

A second problem that arises when we discuss male deference towards women or female deference towards men is that we tend to consider one category of women or men only and incorrectly to extend their behaviour patterns to the total population. For instance, a wife may be very deferent towards her husband, but her son-in-law may be extremely deferent towards his mother-in-law. If, in addition, the wife acquires a son-in-law approximately at the time of marriage (even before the birth of a daughter), as was the case in some traditional African societies, which sex, in that case, is deferent to the other? Obviously, the question is nonsensical, and it is simply a reflection of the supremacy of spousal relationships over other kin relationships in Western societies which have allowed us to state that women are, in general, deferring towards men. Instead, we should specify which category of women defers to which categories of men and women, and which category of men defers to which categories of women and men. Among the Rundi, in Burudi, for example, wives defer greatly to their husbands. However,

A woman who has just served her husband his dinner from a humble, kneeling position, on leaving the house, gives haughty, authoritative commands to the men who work for her. Like any other superior, a woman as the mistress of her house, as a mother, and as an elder sister, commands and punishes. She is respected, she chooses her favourites, and her inferiors ask her for presents. When her role is that of an inferior, she must be obedient, she must work, she must ask for presents, she tries to win the affection of her superior, and she is jealous of those who receive presents. (Albert, 1971, p.192)

The situation is somewhat different with respect to male authority over females. There is a fair bit of evidence that women in industrialised nations have less authority than men, as indicated, for example, by the virtual exclusion of women from the decision-making processes in important political and economic structures in complex societies. But is this also true for women in primitive societies? We have seen above that it is possible to interpret the prevalence of female sexual taboos as a sign of power rather than powerlessness on the part of women. If this is the case, are we then not dealing with two distinct forms of power, a male and a female one? Just as there are labours which are seen as appropriate for men and others which are seen as appropriate for women so there may be forms of power and authority which are seen as appropriate for men and others which are seen as appropriate for women. Lebeuf (1971) who has studied the participation of African women in public affairs comes to just that conclusion. She argues that

    ... the profound philosophical ideas which underlie the assignment of separate tasks to men and women stress the complementarity rather than the separate nature of these tasks. Neither the division of labour nor the nature of the tasks accomplished implies any superiority of the one over the other, and there is almost always compensation in some other direction for the actual inequalities which result from such a division. (Lebeuf, 1971, p.114)

In a culture in which society and nature are perceived in terms of polar opposites which coincide with sexual categories it may not make sense to state that men have greater authority than women — stead, we should specify in which matters men have greater authority than women and in which matters women have greater authority than men. It is only when a norm of sexual equality emerges that we find the emergence of inferiority of women or of male authority over women.

There are now several studies which chart the process through which, counter to conventional wisdom of the sociology of modernisation and industrialisation, the status of women in traditional societies has declined with the advent of Western civilisation. Lebeuf has noted that women in Africa have suffered more from the imposition of colonial systems upon traditional structures than men since they now find themselves systematically excluded from any participation in the new institutional structures (Lebeuf, 1971, p.94). Gaskell (1974) has traced the process of this replacement in one particular culture, in Botswana, and Boserup (1970) has charted the diminution and eventual loss of the traditional authority of women due to industrialisation in developing societies in general. To state, as Smelser has recently done, that the differentiation of economic activities and of family activities which take place during the process of modernisation results in 'the changing status of women, who become generally less subordinated economically, politically, and socially to their husbands than under earlier conditions' (Smelser, 1973, p.273) means to misinterpret completely the position of women in both primitive and complex societies.

Over all, there is no evidence that the 'impressive cross-cultural regularities' that Mussen mentions can be seen as applicable to cultures at different levels of technological development. None of the statements have been found to apply to primitive societies, and only some of them have been found to be descriptive of industrialised nations. This means that we have to modify our notions about male/female polarities in sex roles. Schematically, Table 2.2 summarises the discussion so far.

The Inadequacy of the Sex Roles Approach

In the beginning of the chapter we identified sex role socialisation as a systematic training for acceptance of a double standard. Before discussing the over-all inadequacy of the sex roles approach, we need to somewhat qualify this statement. It is conceivable that a society existed in which women and men had entirely different behaviour expectations for each other and themselves, in which the labour was rigidly divided by sex, but in which nevertheless no subordination of one sex by the other was involved. In such a case, the sexes would be equivalent, although unequal, and in such case it would be misleading to label such sex segregation as an indication of a double standard. Such societies are not very likely to exist, since differentiation tends to lead to stratification, but it is possible that such arrangements could be

Table 2.2: Summary of Purported Cross-cultural Regularities in Sex Differences

	Ideology of Sex Role Behaviour for:		Dichotomies Applicable for:	
Women	Men		Primitive Societies	Complex Societies
—	Strenuous work		No	No
—	Dangerous work		No	No
Repetitive tasks	—		No	No
Stationary } Inside }	Ambulatory } Outside }		No	Upper-class ideal
Minister to needs of others	—		No	Yes
Expressive family roles	Instrumental family roles		No	No
Powerless	Authority over women		No	Yes

found at a lower level of organisation, such as a communal group or some type of family. Situations, then, in which there is absolute equivalence in spite of differentiation can be removed from this discussion. Possibly, the Shakers may provide an example of sex differentiation without stratification.

We have argued that it is possible to distinguish between ten possible versions of the same sex role and that, since this plurality of sex roles is usually ignored, this leads to predictable types of confusion, namely the equating of the ideal with the actual role, the ignoring of the female perception of sex roles, and the equation of the male perception with male and female actual sex role behaviours. We then gave an example of the overextension of the male sex role perception. What is important in this example is that the female perception of her role is not only ignored — the male view is simply seen as the only possible view, so that whatever bias there is must be regarded as an unconscious rather than a conscious bias. There is no indication that any other perspective could be possible, that the view presented is not, in fact, the only true, 'objective' viewpoint.

Then, we looked at purportedly universal cross-cultural regularities in terms of sex roles which are widely accepted as such within the literature. (Mussen provided simply a convenient organising focus.) It turned out that if one took a female perspective, i.e. visualised ego as female, the generalisations as put forward could not be upheld. That does not necessarily mean that men do not *think* that they do the ambulatory, dangerous, physically strenuous, instrumental work, for instance, and that they do not *think* that women do the stationary, safe, physically less strenuous, and expressive work. They may very well do so. In that case, we need only identify this as the male perception of male and female work — and as that, it may be correct. The problem, of course, is that the female perception of the male and female work roles is likely to be quite different, and that some 'objective' measure of determining, for example, the danger or safety of a particular type of work, may be discrepant with both the male and the female perception of the danger or safety.

This is a problem that is present in all studies of sex roles. It can be managed by explicitly stating what version of a sex role it is we are discussing at any point of time, but it makes matters fairly complex. We must, furthermore, accept the notion that there may be cases in which there are several versions of the same sex role which have equal claims to (subjective) validity. One example which illustrates this well can be found in Murphy and Murphy (1974, p.68). A Mundurucu term that gave the Murphys some difficulty was the word *wat* which the anthropologists believed for a time to be roughly translatable as 'owner'. Over time it became apparent to them that a better translation was 'person in charge'. What remained confusing to them was that when they asked an informant who was in charge of a particular house or garden, the respondent, if he was a male, would answer with a man's name, but when they asked a female respondent about the same house or garden, she would answer with a woman's name. The Murphys finally concluded that the different responses they received from women and men reflected a basic difference of opinion as to who indeed was in charge. The conclusion we must draw from this is that we must treat all descriptions of sex roles which do not explicitly identify the sex of an informant and/or of the researcher, and which do not discuss possible alternative versions of the same sex role, with extreme caution.

In principle, the problem of multiple versions of the same sex role is, of course, manageable — we need make sure only that we always get a male and female viewpoint and, where possible, some objective measure of the sex role in question. The problem as noted is, therefore, only a problem of application, not a problem in principle. There is, however, a problem with the sex roles approach that is a problem in principle: a sex roles approach has, by necessity, a conservative bias.

This assertion may seem somewhat astonishing, since most people who study the position of women under the heading of sex roles at the present time tend to think of themselves as feminist, tend therefore to be critical of the present sex structure, and tend to advocate the abolition of sex roles. Nevertheless, the concept of sex roles itself has an implicit conservative bias built into it. 'Role' has at least two components: actual behaviour and normative expectations concerning actual behaviour. In order, therefore, to analyse the content of a sex role, we need to discuss the actual behaviour of people and their expectations concerning 'proper' behaviour by sex. A norm is always a 'should' statement, not an 'is' statement, and at *some* point, the 'is' is judged in terms of the 'should'. In primitive societies which, by definition, have only a rudimentary social structure, there is presumably a high degree of consensus concerning the norms, the 'should'. In complex societies, however, we find a very wide divergence with respect to most societal norms. In order to arrive at a coherent description of a sex role, therefore, the 'normalcy' of a particular norm needs to be established at some point in time. There are basically two ways of establishing such a norm: (1) by arbitrarily accepting the statement of some given population as to what is 'normal', and (2) by some statistical criterion of normalcy.

The first way of establishing the normalcy of a norm consists of asking a group of people about their own normative expectations concerning the proper behaviour for women and men, girls and boys, with respect to some given type of situation. Often, for reasons of convenience, these judges tend to be college students, so that sex role norms are probably disproportionately described in terms of the normative expectations of disproportionately well-educated, young, relatively well-to-do people in a somewhat anomic environment. Sometimes, however, other groups of people are asked, and their normative expectations are recorded. We can then identify different sex role expectations with respect to the same situation (e.g. participation of women in the labour market or the parental obligations of fathers) by membership in different groups, e.g. working-class girls, chicano boys, black men, senior citizens, etc. This is, clearly, one step forward from trying to establish *one* norm for an entire complex society, but all it does is to shift the cut-off point somewhat forward. At some point in time, we need to accept the statements of the people who have been asked as truly representative of sex role expectations for either the entire society or for their particular subgroup. At that point, then, we will correlate the norms with actual behaviour and find some congruence and some discrepancy. This is where the problem arises. As we know, attitudes and behaviours are often at a variance with each other. When discussing sex roles, we are searching for a gauge for actual behaviour, and ultimately, therefore, actual behaviour will be evaluated in terms of some norm (i.e. ideal behaviour). This leads to the paradox that behaviour that is, indeed, widespread and accepted as a fact of life may be classified as deviant because it does not match some abstract norm. This is, for instance, the case with the participation of women in the labour market. There has throughout history been a substantial portion of women who have worked for pay. However, there has also been an upper-class and, by now, middle-class ideal that women should not work for pay. By focusing on this norm which is, it is true, held by a substantial portion of people, a well-accepted alternative pattern has suddenly been identified as, not an alternate pattern but a deviant pattern.

The second manner of defining normalcy is substantially similar, but arrived at in a different manner. Instead of accepting the statement of some real group of people with respect to sex role norms as normative, a statistical distribution is utilised to establish a pattern of normalcy. No matter what the statistical procedure used, the people at the extreme endpoints of the distribution become by definition abnormal, deviant. For example, female loggers and male homemakers are extremely rare. They are, statistically speaking, deviations, abnormal. However, in terms of their work behaviour, female loggers and male homemakers may be identical to male loggers and female homemakers; in addition, they may be well accepted by their co-workers. (For the sake of argument, let us assume that this is the case.) Irrespective of their identical work behaviour and their, let us assume, identical performance and good acceptance by their co-workers, these people would still be defined as abnormal, atypical, deviant. Statistically, of course, this is true. However, by expressing it in this manner (logging is not part of the female role, and homemaking is not part of the male role) we accept sex as a relevant criterion for making such an allocation of labour, when, in fact, the people affected (the female logger and her co-workers, and the male homemaker, his neighbours and his family) find the situation highly acceptable. In short, sex roles may be rigidified through being studied, and through being projected onto other sectors of society.

In this process, there is a dialetic operative. We need, at some point in time, simply to document existing attitudes, and to chart behaviours as they are differentiated by sex. If, however, we continue to do so routinely, what could have been the starting-point for change will become a factor in retarding social change. After having made some inventory of sex roles within a society, we need to proceed to analyse the behaviours of women and men by variables other than sex, e.g. we need to explain the behaviours exhibited by housewives not by some sex-related variable, but by their work conditions, which is a variable equally applicable to women and men. Only when focusing on non-sexual variables will we be able to identify factors that can, potentially, be changed.

Over all, sex roles are a concept that make sense only in a (numerically) larger context. Consequently, when sex roles are discussed, especially in societies other than our own (whichever one that may be), they tend to be discussed in terms of their functionality for some other, larger, unit or system, such as the family. the community, the society. Since all social units, including the family, community and society are presently partially based on some sort of sex role differentiation, it is a truism to state that the sex roles, as they happen to be at a given point in time, need to be preserved because otherwise these larger units or systems would all be changed. Therefore, sex roles tend to be discussed in terms of their functionality for some larger system, rather than in terms of their functionality for individual people. By perceiving the importance of sex roles for the maintenance of, say, the family, we become insensitive to the injustice that is done to the individual people who make up the various families. What is eufunctional for a family, tribe, clan, community, society, need certainly not be eufunctional for individuals. The notion of sex roles by itself gives us no guidance as to what aspects of a given sex role constellation are more or less beneficial or harmful to specific groups of individuals. When we use instead of sex roles the concept of the double standard, we are fundamentally questioning the appropriateness of using sex as a discriminatory factor, since the basic notion behind the double standard is that in identical situations identical consequences should accrue to both sexes, and that differences should only be there when sex does make a difference, when, in other words, the situations are *not* identical. In that sense, the concept of the double standard can, potentially, provide us with guidelines as to what are acceptable sex differences and what are unacceptable differences: whenever we can show that at the individual or aggregate level identical exertions are differentially rewarded, we have an illegitimate sex difference; when, on the other hand, we find differences that are grounded in biological sex differences, we have a legitimate sex difference. To give one last example in this context: if employers were to specify the requirements for becoming a logger not in terms of the sex of an applicant, but in terms of some physical characteristic — stamina, capacity to withstand great cold, capacity to lift certain amounts of weight, etc. — and it so happened that a disproportionately large percentage of applicants and, therefore, hired employees was female or male, we need not be concerned, for, *as long as the requirements are a necessary aspect of the job*, there is no double standard involved. Admittedly, this is a touchy issue, and people may disagree whether a requirement (e.g. height requirements for police officers) is in fact necessary. Nevertheless, the burden of proof would be on the employer to defend the relevance of all requirements. Along with members of one sex, members of the other sex would also be disqualified, but we would not rule out from competition those members of the minority sex (in this context) who meet the necessary standards. Sex has, by this procedure, become irrelevant and any sex difference found is, by definition, a legitimate one.

Notes

1. There is an ongoing debate within the sociology of the family as to what constitutes the best (or a good) measure of family power — with little agreement so far to be seen. The most interesting aspect of the debate in our context is not the apparently major issue, namely what is the best (or a good) measure of family power, but a side issue, namely the assumption that it is possible to find *one* measure of family power that adequately expresses both female and male power. This assumption manifests itself in two major ways: first, often only one spouse, usually the wife, is questioned about family power. This is still a prevalent practice and has been sharply criticised by Safilios-Rothschild (1969). Second, if researchers do ask both spouses and find discrepancies in the responses, the discrepancy is usually explained as a methodological weakness in the particular measure employed (e.g. Scanzoni, 1965, pp. 109-15, or Wilkening and Morrison, 1963, p.351). One researcher who noted that half of the couples interviewed in his study gave conflicting answers to the question of who usually wins in disagreements (Turk, 1975, p.248) concluded that this was an indication that the measure employed did not constitute a satisfactory approach to the measurement of family power. Alternatively, the researcher may treat the perception of one spouse as more correct than that of the other (by implication the perception of one spouse is regarded as not adequately reflecting reality, with the researcher deciding which perspective is 'true' or 'correct') (cf. Heer, 1962). By contrast, Safilios-Rothschild (1969, p.291) suggests that the reason for discrepancies between the husbands' and wives' responses may be the 'possibility of two "realities", the husband's subjective reality and the wife's subjective reality — two perspectives which do not always coincide'. Obviously, it is more interesting and appropriate to consider the discrepancies in the perceptions of spouses as a phenomenon to be noted and investigated rather than as a background noise which needs to be eliminated.

2. Another manifestation of the double standard in scientific analysis is the custom of asking different questions of the sexes. In the instance considered here, this is done implicitly, by considering only female sexual taboos rather than male and female sexual taboos. This is not an uncommon practice. Murdock in his *Ethnographic Atlas* (1967), for example, has a variable 'Norms for Pre-marital Sex Behaviour of Girls' but no corresponding variable on norms for pre-marital behaviour of boys. In other cases, women and men are asked different questions concerning the same topic; for obvious reasons the researcher then receives different responses, which, in turn, are interpreted to indicate the presence of a sex difference.

3. The major causes of fatal accidents in modern complex societies tend to be transport accidents in motor vehicles and home accidents. In Canada in 1956, 2,179 fatalities occurred in the home, which compares with 155 fatalities in mine and quarry, and 423 in industry in the same year. (Statistics Canada, 84-513 Fatal Accidents: Mortality Summary, 1959). This seems to be a relatively typical home accident fatality rate: in Canada in 1956 the home accident fatality rate per 100,000 population was 13.6, in England in 1955 it was 12.9 and in the United States in 1955 it was 13.9 (ibid., p. 5). The over-all picture with respect to injuries is similar: in Canada in 1956, 43.5 per cent of non-transport injuries occurred in the home, compared to 10.0 per cent of non-transport injuries which occurred in industrial premises, mines, and quarries (ibid., p.20, draft 4).

4. Between 1961 and 1973 inclusive, the total battle deaths of US military forces in Vietnam was 46,163 (US Bureau of the Census, Statistical Abstract of the United States: 1974 (95th edn), Washington, DC, 1974, no. 510, p.317). By

comparison, 46,200 people died in the USA *in 1974 alone* in motor vehicle accidents. When considering these figures it should be borne in mind that 1974 has the lowest death-rate on record in the USA, due to the energy crisis and economic recession (Accident Facts (1975 edn), Published by the National Safety Council, Chicago, p.3).

5. Cf. footnote 3. The rate of males reporting home injuries per 1,000 population was, in the age category 25-44, 26 in Canada in 1950/1. For females, the corresponding rate was 45, suggesting that females are differentially exposed to a higher risk of home accidents (Canadian Sickness Survey, 1950-1, Ottawa, Queen's Printer, 1961, Table 19).

6. The pertinent categories are as follows:

| | Workday | | | | Day-off | | | |
| | Women | | Men | | Women | | Men | |
	No Child	Child	No Child	Child	No Child	Child	No Child	Child
Necessary Travel	1.0	1.0	1.4	1.4	0.7	0.7	0.9	1.1
Regular Shopping	0.9	0.8	0.1	0.1	0.2	0.2	0.1	0.1
Visiting	0.7	0.8	0.5	0.4	1.2	1.3	0.9	1.1
	2.6	2.6	2.0	1.9	2.1	2.2	1.9	2.3

Adapted from Meissner, Humphreys, Meis, Scheu (1975), p.434, Table IV.

7. The instrumental/expressive leadership hypothesis in the family has been criticised, among others, by Lipman-Blumen (1976), Leik (1963), Smith (1973), Laws (1971), and Levinger (1964). The combined work of Burke (1972), Lipman-Blumen (1976), Leik (1963), and Smith (1973), suggests that a dual leadership role along an expressive/instrumental dimension should evolve in (1) laboratory groups, (2) of all male members, (3) of the same age, (4) previously unacquainted, (5) of middle-class background, who are (6) given tasks that can be described as having low legitimacy, and (7) inspiring low levels of motivation and then asked after each session to (8) rank each other and themselves on various factors including instrumental dimensions and 'best liked' and who, as a group, (9) show high consensus on the contributions of the members. In as far as the family does not correspond to these conditions the presence of the expressive/instrumental leadership specialisation has not been empirically shown to exist — its existence has been simply asserted (cf. Laws, 1971).

References

Albert, Ethel M. 'Women of Burundi: A Study of Social Values', in Denise Paulme (ed.), *Women of Tropical Africa* (Berkeley and Los Angeles, University of California Press, 1971), pp. 179-216.
Bales, Robert F. and Philip E. Slater, 'Role Differentiation in Small Decision-Making Groups', in Talcott Parsons and Robert F. Bales (eds.), *Family, Social-*

ization and Interaction Process (USA, Free Press of Glencoe, 1955), pp. 259-306.

de Beauvoir, Simone. *The Second Sex* (New York, Bantam, 1952).

Bernard, Jessie. *The Future of Marriage* (New York, Bantam, 1972).

Boserup, Ester. *Woman's Role in Economic Development* (New York, St. Martin's Press, 1970).

Boyd, Monica, Margrit Eichler and John Hofley, 'Family:Functions, Formation and Fertility', in Gail C.A. Cook (ed.), *Opportunity for Choice* (Ottawa, Statistics Canada in association with the C.D. Howe Research Institute, 1976), pp.13-52.

Burke, P.J. 'Leadership Role Differentiation', in C.G. McClintock (ed.), *Experimental Social Psychology* (New York, Holt, Rinehart and Winston, 1972).

Cumming, Elaine, Charles Lazer and Lynne Chisholm. 'Suicide as an Index of Role Strain among Employed and Not Employed Married Women in British Columbia', in *Canadian Review of Sociology and Anthropology* vol. 12, no. 4 (part 1) (1975), pp. 462-70.

D'Andrade, R. 'Sex Differences and Cultural Institutions', in Eleanor Maccoby (ed.), *The Development of Sex Differences* (Stanford, California, Stanford University Press, 1966), pp. 173-203.

Devereux, George. 'The Psychology of Feminine Genital Bleeding: An Analysis of Mohave Indian Puberty and Menstrual Rites', *International Journal of Psycho-Analysis*, vol. 31 (1950), pp.237-57.

Eichler, Margrit. 'Power and Sexual Fear in Primitive Societies', *Journal of Marriage and the Family*, vol. 37, no. 4 (1975), pp. 917-26.

Evans-Pritchard, E.E. *Man and Woman among the Azande* (London, Faber and Faber, 1974).

Ford, Clellan S. 'Some Primitive Societies', in Georgene H. Seward and Robert C. Williamson (eds.), *Sex Roles in Changing Society* (New York, Random House, 1970), pp.25-43.

Gaskell, Jane. 'The Participation of Women in the Adult Education Programmes of Botswana', (paper presented at the Canadian Sociology and Anthropology Meetings, Toronto, 1974).

Heer, David M. 'Husband and Wife Perceptions of Family Power Structure', *Marriage and Family Living*, vol. 24, (1962), pp.65-7.

Kanter, Rosabeth Moss. 'Women and the Structure of Organizations: Explorations in Theory and Behavior', in Marcia Millman and Rosabeth Moss Kanter (eds.), *Another Voice. Feminist Perspectives on Social Life and Social Science* (New York, Garden City, 1975),pp. 34-74.

Laws, Judith. 'A Feminist Review of Marital Adjustment Literature: The Rape of the Locke', *Journal of Marriage and the Family*, vol. 33, (1971), pp. 483-516.

Lebeuf, Annie M.D. 'Role of Women in the Political Organizations of African Societies', in Denise Paulme (ed.), *Women of Tropical Africa* (Berkeley and Los Angeles, University of California Press, 1971), pp.93-120.

Leik, R.K. 'Instrumentality and Emotionality in Family Interaction', *Sociometry*, vol. 26 (1963), pp.131-45.

Levinger, George. 'Task and Social Behaviour in Marriage', *Sociometry*, vol. 27 (1964), pp.433-48.

Linton, R. *The Cultural Background of Personality* (New York, Appleton-Century-Crofts, 1945).

Lipman-Blumen, Jean and Ann Tickamyer. 'Sex Roles in Transition: A Ten-Year Perspective', *Annual Review of Sociology*, vol. 1 (1976).

Maccoby, Eleanor and Carol N. Jacklin. *The Psychology of Sex Differences* (Stanford, California, Stanford University Press, 1974).

Maranda, Elli K. 'A Woman is an Alien Spirit', in C.J. Matthiasson (ed.), *Many*

58   *The Double Standard in Behaviour Expectations*

Sisters (New York, Free Press, 1974), pp.177-202.

Meissner, Martin *et al*. 'No Exit for Wives: Sexual Division of Labour and the Cumulation of Household Demands', *Canadian Review of Sociology and Anthropology*, vol. 12, no. 4 (part 1) (1975), pp.424-39.

Murdock, George P. 'Comparative Data on the Division of Labour by Sex', *Social Forces*, vol. 15, no. 4 (Oct.-May 1936-7) pp. 551-3.

Murdock, George P. *Social Structure* (New York, Free Press, 1965).

Murdock, George P. *Ethnographic Atlas* (Pitsburgh, University of Pittsburgh Press, 1967).

Murphy, Yolanda and Robert F. Murphy. *Women of the Forest* (New York and London, Columbia University Press, 1974).

Mussen, Paul H. 'Early Sex-Role Development' in David A. Goslin (ed.), *Handbook of Socialization Theory Research* (1969) pp. 707-31.

Neff, Wanda F. *Victorian Working Women. An Historical and Literary Study of Women in British Industries and Professions 1832-1850* (London, Frank Cass and Co., 1966).

Papanek, Hanna. 'Purdah in Pakistan: Seclusion and Modern Occupations for Women', *Journal of Marriage and the Family*, vol. 33 (1971), pp.517-30.

Parsons, Talcott, 'Family Structures and the Socialization of the Child', in Talcott Parsons and Robert F. Bales (eds.), *Family, Socialization and Interaction Process* (Glencoe, Illinois, Free Press, 1955).

Parsons, Talcott, Edward A. Shils and James Olds. 'Values, Motives and Systems of Action', in Talcott Parsons and Edward A. Shils (eds.), *Toward a General Theory of Action* (Cambridge, Massachusetts, Harvard University Press, 1951), pp. 47-278.

Pleck, Joseph H. and Jack Sawyer (eds.). *Men and Masculinity* (Englewood Cliffs, New Jersey, Prentice-Hall, 1974).

Safilios-Rothschild, Constantina. 'Family Sociology or Wives' Family Sociology? A Cross-Cultural Examination of Decision-Making', *Journal of Marriage and the Family* (1969), pp.290-301.

Scanzoni, John. 'A Note on the Sufficiency of Wife Responses in Family Research', *Pacific Sociological Review* (Fall 1965), pp.109-15.

Silverman, Erwin, 'The Experimenter, A (Still) Neglected Stimulus Object', *Canadian Psychologist,* vol. 15, no. 3 (1974), pp.258-70.

Slater, Philip. *The Pursuit of Loneliness. American Culture at the Breaking Point* (Boston, Beacon Press, 1970).

Smelser, Neil J. 'Toward a Theory of Modernization', in Amitai Etzioni and Eva Etzioni-Halevy (eds.), *Social Change, Sources, Patterns and Consequences* (2nd ed.) (New York, Basic Books, 1973), pp. 268-84.

Smith, Dorthy. 'Women, the Family and Corporate Capitalism', in Marylee Stephenson (ed.), *Women in Canada* (Toronto, New Press, 1973), pp.2-35.

Stearns, Peter N. 'Working-Class Women in Britain, 1890-1914', in Martha Vicinus (ed.), *Suffer and Be Still. Women in the Victorian Age* (Bloomington and London, Indiana University Press, 1973, pp.100-20.

Stephens, William N. 'A Cross-Cultural Study of Menstrual Taboos', in *Genetic Psychology Monographs*, vol. 64 (1961), pp.385-416.

Stephens, William N. *The Oedipus Complex. Cross-Cultural Evidence* (New York, Free Press of Glencoe, 1962).

Sullerot, Evelyne. *Die emanzipierte Sklawin, Geschichte und Soziologie der Frauenarbeit* (Wien, Köln, Graz, Hermann Bohlaus Nachf., 1972).

Thomas, Edwin J. and Bruce J. Biddle. 'Basic Concepts for Classifying the Phenomena of Role', in Bruce J. Biddle and Edwin J. Thomas (eds.), *Role Theory: Concepts and Research* (New York, John Wiley, 1966), pp.23-45.

Turk, James L. 'Who has the Power?' in S. Parvez Wakil (ed.), *Marriage, Family and Society. Canadian Perspectives* (Toronto, Butterworth, 1975), pp.237-56.

Wilkening, W.A. and Denton M. Morrison, 'A Comparison of Husband and Wife Responses concerning who makes Farm and Home Decision', *Marriage and Family Living,* vol. 25 (August 1963), pp.349-51.

Wood, David. *Conflict in the Twentieth Century* (Adelphi Paper no. 48) (London, Institute for Strategic Studies, 1968).

Young, F. and A. Bacadayan (sic). 'Menstrual Taboos and Social Rigidity', *Ethnology,* vol. 4 (1965), pp.225-40.

Young, Frank W. and Albert Bacdayan, 'Menstrual Taboos and Social Rigidity', in Clellan S. Ford (ed.), *Cross-Cultural Approaches. Readings in Comparative Research* (New Haven, HRAF Press, 1967), pp.95-110.

Zelditch, Morris, Jr. 'Role Differentiation in the Nuclear Family: A Comparative Study', in Talcott Parsons and Robert F. Bales (eds.), *Family, Socialization and Interaction Process* (USA, Free Press of Glencoe, 1955), pp.307-52.

3 THE DOUBLE STANDARD INTERNALISED: THE INADEQUACY OF THE SEX IDENTITY APPROACH

We have seen that sex roles are universal in their existence, but that their content varies considerably between different societies. Just as every society has sex roles, so every individual has a sex identity. People are taught to conform to sex roles through a process of differential rewards and punishments for so-called sex-appropriate or sex-inappropriate behaviours. In this way, they are socialised into their sex roles. Eventually such behaviour expectations are internalised and become part of their self-image as a woman or a man, a boy or a girl. According to Money and Ehrhardt (1974, p.4) who prefer to use the term gender rather than sex[1], gender identity is 'the private experience of gender role, and gender role is the public expression of gender identity'.

Since the two concepts, sex role and sex identity, are inextricably tied up with each other, theoretically as well as in practice, we would expect to encounter difficulties with the concept of sex identity which are similar to those found with the concept of sex roles.

Sex identity in its most narrow sense consists of the self-awareness of people as sexual beings — the capacity to procreate through sexual intercourse and to enjoy one's body in a variety of ways. However, we have seen in the preceding chapter that all societies have a great many behaviour expectations for their members which, although assigned on the basis of sex, are not in any direct manner related to one's sex. To the degree to which these behaviour expectations have been internalised, sex identity encompasses many behaviour expectations which are in no way related to physiological sex differences.

Sex roles which go beyond biologically determined behaviour are based on a double standard. Sex role socialisation consists of systematic training in accepting the double standard. Sex identity which goes beyond an understanding of ourselves as sexual beings consists of the internalisation of the double standard.

Previously, we distinguished between ten possible versions of a sex role. When the culturally accepted sex role images change (i.e. when the ideal version of a sex role changes) this has implications for the sex identity of individuals, due to the close relationship between sex roles and sex identity. One of the consequences of the women's liberation movement is that many aspects of the prevailing ideal female sex role have been rejected. In consciousness-raising groups, participants are made aware of internalised sex role images, which are then explicitly declared undesirable and illegitimate. A similar process has been taking place in the men's liberation movement.

> Male liberation calls for men to free themselves of the sex role stereotypes that limit their ability to be human. Sex role stereotypes say that men should be dominant; achieving and enacting a dominant role in relations with others is often taken as an indicator of success. 'Success', for a man, often involves influence over the lives of other persons. But success in achieving positions of dominance and influence is necessarily not open to every man, as dominance is relative and hence scarce by definition. Most men fail to achieve the positions of dominance that sex role stereotypes ideally call for. Stereotypes tend to identify such men as greater or lesser failures, and in extreme cases, men who fail to be dominant are the object of jokes, scorn, and sympathy from wives, peers, and society generally . . .
>
> Male liberation seeks to aid in destroying the sex role stereotypes that regard 'being a man' and 'being a woman' as statuses that must be achieved through proper behavior. People need not take on restrictive roles to establish their sexual identity. (Sawyer, 1976, pp.287-8)

This process is important, because sex roles are internalised to the degree that we consider a woman behaving in a feminine manner or a man behaving in a masculine manner just 'natural'. An individual cannot change the social expectations that are applied to his or her sex, but a social movement potentially may, and an individual can change his or her acceptance of the legitimacy of a prevailing set of sex-related behaviour expectations.

In order to change sex roles at the social level and one's own understanding of one's sex identity at the personal level, those ideal sex role expectations which have been internalised must be made explicit. This is a necessary process, but one which has its own peculiar dangers. In order to be able to reject an ideal sex role, we must first prove its existence and prevalence, so that we can then repudiate it. In the process of proving its existence and prevalence, a reification may set in in which we treat the ideal sex role as if it represented the actual behaviours of women and men. In other words, we confuse the ideal and actual versions of the sex role by neglecting the fact that at no time do people ever live up to the ideal version of any role. At best (or at worst) they approximate them. There are always variations by social stratum and by other variables. By treating the ideal sex role as if at some point in time, it had ever been the actual sex role, we may, ironically, strengthen the very cultural ideal that we wish to eliminate. Attempting to change an ideal sex role by a process of repudiation implies that we remain antithetically tied to what we wish to overcome.

Feminist scholars and thinkers have for some time been aware of the danger of using only a negative ideal as a normative guide. The concept of androgyny (which literally means male-femaleness) has been introduced as the new, positive, cultural ideal for behaviour that is not tied to previously existing sex role limitations. Yet, for as long as we continue to measure ourselves against a positive or negative norm of sex-appropriate behaviour, we shall never overcome the limitations of sex roles and of a sex identity that is tied to a pervasive system of sex roles. Paradoxically, the literature dealing with androgyny and with sex identity, while explicitly attempting to overcome current limitations of sex roles and sex identity, nevertheless contributes to and even cements their continued existence. We shall now examine in more detail how this comes about.

A Critique of Masculinity-Femininity Scales

When discussing sex identity, we can discuss a variety of processes and traits: the development of sex identity, the continued reassurance of one's sex identity, the range of possible sex identities, etc. In any case, however, we reach at some time the point where we have to define, and ultimately operationalise so that it can be measured, the crucial variable: sex identity. The prevalent manner of measuring sex identity is through masculinity-femininity scales (M-F scales). To understand and critically to evaluate the meaning of M-F scales is, therefore, central to an understanding of the whole literature on sex identity.

There are several such scales in existence. Probably the best of these, and a very widely used one, is the Bem Sex Roles Inventory (BSRI) (Bem, 1974). This scale avoids one of the greatest problems of its predecessors by not scoring a high masculinity item as a low femininity item and vice versa; in other words, it is not based on the assumption that masculinity and femininity are two mutually exclusive personality characteristics.

In order to understand the problems underlying all masculinity-femininity scales we need to scrutinise the manner in which the BSRI was constructed. Judges were asked to rate 400 personality characteristics on a scale from 1 to 7 ('not at all desirable' to 'extremely desirable'). For instance, each individual judge was asked to rate the items 'in American society, how desirable is it for a man to be truthful?' or 'in American society, how desirable is it for a woman to be sincere?' from 1 to 7. Each individual judge rated the desirability of all 400 personality characteristics either for a man or for a woman, never for both. A personality characteristic was identified as masculine if it was independently judged by both male and female judges to be more desirable for a man than for a woman and, conversely, it was identified as feminine if it was judged to be more desirable for a woman than for a man. Of the characteristics which satisfied these criteria, 20 were selected to construct a masculinity scale, 20 to construct a femininity scale, and 20 to construct a neutral scale. Since the neutral scale does not enter into the computation of the final M-F scores, it will be ignored here.

The 20 masculine and 20 feminine items that make up the masculine and feminine scales are shown in Table 3.1.

Table 3.1: Masculinity and Femininity Scales of the BSRI

Masculine items	Feminine items
Acts as a leader	Affectionate
Aggressive	Cheerful
Ambitious	Childlike
Analytical	Compassionate
Assertive	Does not use harsh language
Athletic	Eager to soothe hurt feelings
Competitive	Feminine
Defends own beliefs	Flatterable
Dominant	Gentle
Forceful	Gullible
Has leadership abilities	Loves children
Independent	Loyal
Individualist	Sensitive to needs of others
Makes decisions easily	Shy
Masculine	Soft-spoken
Self-reliant	Sympathetic
Self-sufficient	Tender
Strong personality	Understanding
Willing to take a stand	Warm
Willing to take risks	Yielding

In order to find an individual's M-F score, a person ranks himself or herself on all masculine and feminine items on a 7-point scale from 'never or almost never true' to 'always or almost always true'. On the basis of these self-ratings, a person receives three scores: a masculinity score, a femininity score, and an androgyny score. The masculinity score equals the mean self-rating for all endorsed masculine items, the femininity score equals the self-rating for all endorsed feminine items. Both masculinity and femininity scores are logically independent, i.e. they can vary independently (you may be high on masculinity and low on femininity, or high on both, or low on both, etc.). The androgyny score is based on the M-F scores, on the other hand. It is computed as the difference between an individual's masculinity and femininity normalised with respect to the standard deviations of his or her masculinity and femininity scores. In other words, the closer the score is to zero, the more androgynous is the person according to this measure.

The basic problem underlying the construction of these scales is one which is parallel to the problem found in women's and men's consciousness-raising groups: the reification of sex role stereotypes. The stereotype takes on a life of its own, becomes normative, and empirical reality is measured and evaluated against this norm. Reality has been stood on its head.

There are several aspects to this reification of sex role stereotypes through M-F scales. The first is the role of the judges. It is clear, in the way in which the original question was phrased (in American society, how desirable is it for a man to be ... ?) that judges were asked to respond in terms of their perception of a generalised public, not in terms of their own personal view of reality. (They are emphatically *not* asked how desirable do *you* think it is for a man to be ...) This is likely to build in a peculiar conservative bias. There is some evidence that respondents tend to assign more conservative attitudes to other people than they themselves hold.

Apparently, there is a relatively sharp break between what people perceive to be a cultural norm and what they accept as guidelines for their own actions, or, in our terminology, between the ideal male and female roles and the actual male and female roles. There is some indication that this process of differentiation may start at a very early date. In a recent experiment involving toy choices, five- to six-year-old children were asked to choose which toy they would prefer to play with from matched pairs of toys which had previously been identified as more or less feminine or masculine by adult judges (education students). Following the first toy preference test, the children were divided into three groups, one of which received an androgynous roles lesson, one which received a traditional roles lesson, and a control group which did not receive any lesson. Not surprisingly, the toy choices of the children who had received the androgynous roles lesson became less sex-stereotyped in a second and third toy preference test, and those who had not received any treatment stayed essentially the same. Surprisingly, however, the children who had received fairly heavy direct sex role reinforcement also made less sex-stereotyped choices at the second and third occasions. Moreover, the traditional sex roles lesson involved, among other things, a sorting of toys according to sex (doll to girl, boxing glove to boy, etc.), and the children did well in the task as specified, and, furthermore, seemed to enjoy doing it. Nevertheless, their own personal preferences changed into a direction of less sex-stereotyped toys. This indicates that children of age five to six are already capable of making a clear distinction between what they see as the cultural norm concerning 'sex-appropriate' toys, but they do not feel bound to abide by the norm when given the chance to make their own free choices. (cf. Laurie, 1977).

Other studies show a similar disjunction between the perceived ideal male and female role and one's own beliefs on this issue. For instance, in a recent nation-wide Canadian opinion survey, people were asked to respond to the statement that women (men) 'tend to be emotional, tend to be practical, tend to be trustworthy, tend to be aggressive, tend to be steady workers, tend to be physically fit' (Decision Marketing Research Limited, 1976, pp.187 and 121-2). The respondents were asked to rate each statement on a scale from 1 to 7, with 4 indicating that they considered the sexes to be equal, 1 indicating that they considered the statement much more applicable to the average woman than the average man, and 7 indicating the reverse. After being asked about their personal feelings, respondents were, in a split sample, asked to comment on how they thought members of their own sex and members of the other sex would feel about these statements. We can thus compare the actual female perception with the female perception of a generalised female population, the female perception of a generalised male population, the actual male perception, the male perception of a generalised female population and, lastly, the male perception of a generalised male population. The differences between the projective questions and the personal statements are quite considerable, with women considering men more conservative than they really are (cf. columns 3 and 4) and men considering women slightly more conservative than they really are (cf. columns 6 and 1).

It is quite likely, therefore, that the designation of character traits as

Table 3.2: Average Scores of Men and Women Concerning Sex
Stereotypes

| | Women | | | | Men | |
	1	2	3	4	5	6
	How Women Feel	How Women Think Other Women Feel	How Women Think Men Feel	How Men Feel	How Men Think Other Men Feel	How Men Think Women Feel
Emotional	2.5	2.6	2.3	2.5	2.5	2.9
Practical	3.4	3.5	4.4	3.8	4.2	3.7
Trustworthy	3.8	3.9	4.3	3.9	4.1	3.8
Aggressive	4.5	4.6	4.7	4.6	4.9	4.7
Steady Workers	4.2	4.2	4.9	4.3	4.5	4.3
Physically Fit	4.1	4.1	4.9	4.1	4.4	4.2

Source: Decision Marketing Research Limited, *Women in Canada* (Toronto,
Office of the Co-ordinator, Status of Women, 2nd edn, 1976, p.122.)

masculine or feminine is more marked on the BSRI than it would have
been had the question been 'how desirable do *you* think it is for a
woman to be ...' In itself, this probable conservative bias towards
greater dichotomisation of sex roles need not concern us, if it were
simply a measure of sex role stereotypes, as held at a particular point in
time by a particular type of population. The problem arises in the way
these stereotypic statements are used.

The sex role stereotypes, as established, serve as a gauge for reality,
rather than reality serving as a corrective for the stereotypes. As the
scales become widely used and penetrate the media, the sex role stereotypes that underlie them are enhanced by an aura of scientific credi-
bility. One can now rest assured that it has been scientifically established that all people believe that women should be affectionate,
cheerful, childlike, compassionate, and should not use harsh language,
whereas men should act as leaders, be aggressive, ambitious, analytical,
assertive, athletic, etc. The fact that in important subgroups other, contrary norms obtain — e.g. athleticism in a girls' sports club, or avoid-
ance of harsh language for everybody in certain religious groups — is
lost. The stereotypes have been reinforced through science.

Second, the judges who were asked to rank the items for the construction of the scales consisted of several sets of male and female college students. This introduces a socio-economic, age and educational
bias. The stereotypes of young, highly educated people with relatively

well-to-do parents are seen as an adequate group to provide the norm against which to assess the stereotypes of other groups of people. One wonders, for instance, how the scales would have differed if old, black, working-class men and women had been the original set of judges. Maybe some of the items which are now masculine would have been rated as feminine or neutral, or some of the neutral items as feminine or masculine, etc.

Third, the items which were finally included in the masculinity-femininity scales were only a few out of very many (40 out of 400). One of the criteria for inclusion was precisely that the item be clearly identified as more desirable either for a woman or for a man. We do not know what other criteria influenced the final selection of items, or what the original list of items were. Although the researchers did have a measure of the social desirability of the various items, they apparently did not have any measure for the salience of the various items. That is, we do not know how salient the items included in the M-F scales are compared with other items which are not included to describe the overall personality of a person. Perhaps a person could be more appropriately described with adjectives that are not contained in any of the scales. If this were so, the scales give too much weight to stereotyped personality characteristics. For the assumption underlying their construction is that the sexes do have different personality structures, not similar ones. By contrast, IQ tests are constructed on the assumption that the sexes are equally intelligent. This is reflected in the fact that items are selected such that the over-all mean score for a given group of males and females will be identical and, if it is not, items are omitted or included such that the mean differences between the sexes vanish. When, therefore, IQ tests 'prove' that the sexes are equally intelligent, they do so because they were constructed to do just that.

Lastly, and most importantly, the placement of people on M-F scales results in identifying them as 'feminine', 'masculine' or 'androgynous' in their orientation, and in the process dehumanises them in the sense that it sexifies the attributes used to describe the personalities of the subjects involved. It works like this: the self-ratings of the subjects are measured against the stereotypes of the original judges which have been ossified into the scales.[2]

For instance, let us assume that we have a group of feminists who rate themselves highly on 'masculine' items (e.g. ambitious, analytical, make decisions easily, self-reliant) without rating themselves highly on an equivalent number of feminine items (e.g. childlike, gullible, shy, soft-spoken, yielding), and, on top of that, they consider themselves eminently feminine, since their notion of a woman is different from that which emerges from the stereotypes which are built into the scales. These women will be classified as masculine, rather than as androgynous or feminine, since their own personal definition of femininity which determines their own sex identity is ignored.

For as long as people identify masculinity-femininity scales as adequate reflections of reality, being analytical, independent, individualistic, self-reliant, and self-sufficient will not be seen as human attributes, but as specifically masculine attributes, even if a majority of women were suddenly found to possess these traits. Empirical reality cannot correct the stereotypes, since it is straijt-jacketed into ossified stereotypes in the form of scales. The double standard has found its most sophisticated expression in M-F scales: the actual behaviour of men may be classified as feminine (while the corresponding behaviour for women would be classified as feminine and thereby 'sex-appropriate') rather than allowing the actual behaviour of women and men gradually to change the perception of the norms.

This is how reality is stood on its head. This process creates considerable confusion in terminology. A sex role can be defined as behaviour expectations considered appropriate for one sex or the other. The male sex role is, then, the behaviour expected of a person because he is male and the female sex role the behaviour expected of a female. An androgynous sex role, therefore, is an impossibility. Androgyny means, precisely, that behaviours are *not* circumscribed by sex, and not that they are in equal parts informed by masculine and feminine behaviour expectations. When Bem (1974, pp.158-9) states that 'a "masculine" sex role thus represents not only the endorsement of masculine attributes but the simultaneous rejection of feminine attributes'; 'a "feminine" sex role represents not only the endorsement of feminine attributes but the simultaneous rejection of masculine attributes' and 'an "androgynous" sex role thus represents the equal endorsement of both masculine and feminine attributes' she is confusing the concept of role with the ascription of stereotypic attributes on the part of the researcher to real people, irrespective as to what they see as their sex role or their sex identity.

The concept of androgyny has been introduced to overcome the limitations imposed on people because of their sex. In the social sciences, the concept is used to overcome the limitations of masculinity-femininity distinctions, and among feminists it is widely accepted as a normative ideal. However, once we examine the definitions and operationalisations of androgyny, we can see that it does not overcome the masculine-feminine division, and may, in fact, cement it.[3]

A Critique of the Concept of Androgyny

Until fairly recently, the only socially desirable, and, for many people, the only thinkable social ideal was to be a feminine woman or a masculine man. People who were dissatisfied with the prevailing notion of femininity and masculinity could criticise the content of these two concepts (e.g. a real woman is strong, a real man can show his love, etc.), but they did not question the desirability of being a feminine or masculine being, however it might be defined. The introduction of the concept of androgyny represents an enormous step forward. The concept of psychological androgyny is based on the notion that every person, male and female, has a feminine *and* a masculine side as part of their personality. Androgyny is perceived as a social ideal: only that person who does not repress either side of these two separate poles can be a fully mature personality. In order to achieve this ideal, we must create a society in which social androgyny prevails: a state in which every person, irrespective of sex, can draw on all types of previously sex-stereotyped behaviours, and in which all sorts of opportunities are open to everybody irrespective of his or her sex.

In so far as the concept of androgyny challenges the mutual exclusiveness of masculinity and femininity, whether at the social or at the psychic level, it constitutes a real advance in our thinking. In so far as the concept remains antithetically tied to the concepts of masculinity and femininity, as by necessity it must, it now represents a hurdle that needs to be overcome. When criticising the concept, however, it should be remembered that it was a necessary step in the evolution of non-sexist thought.

If androgyny is measured on the Bem Sex Role Inventory, all the criticisms levelled at the M-F scales apply to androgyny, as well, since the androgyny score is derived from the masculinity and femininity scores. However, the criticism that needs to be undertaken with respect to androgyny is a general one, rather than one geared to a specific type of operationalisation. Androgyny is usually defined as the absence of sex role constraints, i.e. it is usually defined in negative terms. Occasionally, it is defined in positive terms, as the social and psychic condition in which individuals can develop their full potential irrespective of their sex. The negative definition implies that we first define sex role constraints such that we shall be able to notice their absence. We are therefore back to dealing with sex roles. The positive definition implies that we find some criterion by which to measure the degree of development of different individuals's potential such that we can recognise it as different from the development of their potential in a sex-constrained manner. We are again back to dealing with sex roles. No matter which route is taken, the concept of androgyny remains antithetically linked to the concepts of masculinity and femininity − in a truly androgynous society the concept of androgyny would not exist, since sex would be considered an irrelevant variable except where relevant for biological reasons.

For example, we live in a society that is non-chauvinistic in respect of how to eat one's eggs. Correspondingly, we have no concept that divides people into groups according to how they break their eggs. When Gulliver, in his many strange journeys, came to the two empires of Lilliput and Blefuscu (which were inhabited by tiny people) he found that the fierce war that raged between the two empires centred around the issue as to how to break one's eggs, with the Lilliputians relentlessly pursuing all people who broke their egg at the larger end, the Big-Endians, which was contrary to the publicly announced Lilliputian habit of breaking the egg at the smaller end (Swift, 1963, p.37). A truly androgynous society would be just as devoid of the concept of androgyny as we are of the concept of Big-Endian. To recognise the existence of androgynous traits or conditions presupposes the recognition of masculine and feminine traits and conditions. In other words, the concept of androgyny itself reinforces the existence of sex stereotypes, in so far as it reinforces the notion that sex-linked traits do, in fact, exist.

Let us take an example. Let us assume that a man is cheerful, affectionate, loves children, and is understanding. This man will be described as a feminine man, unless he gets equally high scores on some masculine items in which case he will be described as androgynous. A person is described as androgynous only if he or she displays the 'proper' (but entirely arbitrary) combination of masculine and feminine traits. This is the insoluble discrepancy between the positive and negative definitions of androgyny: the negative definition of androgyny as a non-limitation by sex stereotypes which, implicitly, reinforces precisely those stereotypes it has set out to overcome, makes a positive operationalisation in effect impossible. Let us assume that it is a woman who is cheerful, affectionate, gentle, loves children, and is understanding, and that she is, in addition, gifted with all other female-stereotyped traits. This woman will be described as feminine and thereby non-androgynous, although she may fulfil her potential to the very best. The link between androgyny and masculinity-femininity requires a particular combination of character traits for a person to be classified as androgynous, although this combination may be quite inappropriate for that particular person.

Fundamentally, this is a problem of extrapolating from a statistical distribution to individuals. But even if we cease to utilise the concept of an androgynous sex role (which is nonsensical) or of an androgynous personality (which seems to be fraught with more dangers than advantages), androgyny is still a problematic concept. We have never known a society that is devoid of sex roles, neither in our own experience nor in anthropological literature. More importantly, we have never known of a society that is completely devoid of the double standard, although there are great variations with respect to the degree of double standardism. We can talk of a sex role when we observe that members of one sex engage more frequently in a particular type of behaviour (e.g. babysit, or drink at bars) than members of the other sex, and when people come to expect these sex-specific behaviours. We identify these expectations as aspects of the double standard, and thereby as illegitimate only when there is no natural reason why people should have such expectations, and when there is a power differential. For instance, we do not expect normal healthy adults to sit down at table in order to be spoonfed, but we do expect this of toddlers. The reason is a natural reason, and thereby not part of a double standard. By the same token, it is conceivable that a society divides its labour by sex in a fairly rigid manner but in such a way that the sexes are, both individually and as social groups, symmetrically dependent on each other. There would be, thus, no sexual power differential (cf. Eichler, n.d.). While this is unlikely ever to be completely implemented, since social differentiation tends to result in social stratification (Holter, 1970), this situation may be somewhat approximated in some rural societies.

If we postulate, in thought, the existence of a society free of any sexual double standard, it might be that there still would be systematic differences in character traits, behaviours, and subsequently in behaviour expectations between the sexes. This possibility is not allowed for when we conceptualise non-sexism, non-double standardism, as androgyny which understands itself as a combination of masculine and feminine traits and behaviours. In order to overcome the sexual double standard, we need to show that sex is an irrelevant basis on which to make those distinctions which today are still being made between the sexes, and from there to let each person develop as he or she wishes to, without worrying whether this falls on the so-called masculine or so-called feminine side of some fictitious continuum.

Sex Change Operations — The Last Bulwark of the Double Standard

Sex change operations have become increasingly frequent over the past decade. The fact that modern societies are willing to allocate a portion of their scarce resource of highly trained medical personnel and highly sophisticated and expensive medical instruments for such operations suggests a complete acceptance of sex role ideology and therefore an extreme intolerance of sexual ambiguity.

In conventional psychology, people distinguish between people who have a 'sex-appropriate gender identity' and those who have a confused gender identity, or exhibit a 'gender dysphoria syndrome' (Meyer, 1974). Within the last decade, the treatment of people with gender dysphoria, that is, people who believe that they have the wrong-sexed body for their 'real' self, has increasingly been through sex change operations, more commonly referred to in the literature as 'sex reassignment surgery'.

Sex reassignment surgery has as its goal to make a man as much as is anatomically possible similar to a woman, although it can never make a woman out of a man. The intention of the surgery is to make it possible for the erstwhile male to live as much as possible like a woman, and to be accepted as a woman by his (now her) friends and acquaintances. Vice versa, the surgery aims to make a woman as much as is anatomically possible similar to a man, although, again, it can never make a man out of a woman. Again, the surgery is considered successful if the erstwhile woman is accepted and treated as a man by her (now his) friends and acquaintances. In general, sex reassignment surgery is a costly and long process, and the final surgery which gives it its name is only, if responsibly done, the last step in a several years' process of 'changing one's sex' — namely, living in the mode of a member of the opposite sex.

As a rule, transsexualism for a man who wants to become a woman involves, first, hormone treatment, which increases his breast development, effectively sterilises him, and decreases his facial hair growth. A second step would be electrolysis of his facial hair, of his breast hair and, if necessary, of other parts. After the second hair removal, the hair is usually permanently removed. Sometimes a hair transplant to alter his hair line at the forehead and/or a nose operation are performed. Sometimes breast implants are made to increase his breast size beyond the increase that is due to the hormonal treatment. At this point the patient is often expected to live as a woman for a minimum of six months, and, if possible, for several years. Physicians seem to vary greatly in this requirement, but most seem to be more willing to perform the ultimate sex reassignment surgery the longer the patient has already lived as a member of the sex which he wishes to join. The next step, then, is the removal of the penis and the testes and, lastly, the construction of an artificial vagina (vaginoplasty), with which the person is actually capable of having sexual intercourse, assuming the role of the woman, sometimes to such a degree that her partner is unaware of the fact that the person used to be an anatomical male.

For female-to-male transsexuals, the process is even more complicated. As with male-to-female transsexuals, the first medical step is usually hormone treatments. The androgens tend to lower the voice, and to stimulate facial hair growth. After a prolonged period of time, they also effectively sterilise the erstwhile woman, and periods cease, just as the man with a great influx of estrogens becomes incapable of ejaculation. The next step would be the surgical removal of the breasts, and preceding or succeeding it a hysterectomy (removal of the uterus). This is about as far as many female-to-male transsexuals can go, although there is, by now, a technology which allows the construction of a penis (phalloplasty). The construction of a penis by surgical means is more complicated than the removal of the male sex organs and the construction of an artificial vagina: female-to-male transsexuals can receive a penile construction and an implant of simulated testes which look like male genitals, but the penis cannot get erect, and, of course, cannot ejaculate since there are no functioning testes, and often it cannot even be used for urination. For sexual intercourse it seems to be useless (with the exception of one case that has been reported). The surgical changes are, therefore, of an even more cosmetic nature (since still less functional than the artificial vagina) than those of the male-to-female transsexual.

As can be seen, the whole process is by necessity painful, physically as well as emotionally, and expensive. Persons undergoing sex reassignment surgery need to possess a great deal of determination in order to obtain the desired treatments and operations. Nevertheless, there is no doubt that the incidence of these sex reassignment surgeries have greatly increased over the past few years. Money and Wolff (1973) estimated that in 1971 there were around 300 post-operative transsexuals in the United States, and in 1976 Freinbloom estimated that there were about 2,000 post-operative transsexuals in the USA. Overall, Pauly (1974a, p.493) estimates the prevalence of male transsexualism as 1:100,000 and of female transexualism as 1:130,000 of the general population. The lower female transexualism rate may simply be a function of the fact that female-to-male sex reassignment surgery is even more complicated and expensive than male-to-female sex reassignment surgery, and that male transsexualism has received more publicity through some famous cases such as Christine Jorgenson and Jan Morris. Were the possibility of female-to-male surgery better known, more people might request it.

The generic term that is utilised to describe a person who wishes to live as a member of the other sex is 'transsexual'. In the last years, the term has been utilised to designate all those people who seek (but do not necessarily obtain) a sex change operation. The ratio of patients receiving surgery and those requesting it has been estimated as 1:9 (Bentler, 1976, p.577). The usage of calling all patients requesting surgery transsexual has been criticised by Meyer (1974) as being too vague, and he proposes to call transsexual only those people who have actually managed to live as members of the other sex. It is common to distinguish between post-operative and pre-operative transsexuals. This, to me, seems a very questionable custom, since it assumes that all 'pre-operative' transsexuals will, some day, become post-operative, which is not the case. More important, it stresses the surgical aspect of transsexualism rather than the cultural aspect by implying that transsexualism culminates in sex reassignment surgery, and that a form of transsexualism which involves living as a member of the opposite sex without surgery is simply a step to having surgery performed. If nothing else, it indicates the mechanical nature of the way in which gender dysphoria is regarded among the clinical experts.

Related to, but not synonymous with, transsexualism are transvestism and homosexuality. Transvestism involves an acceptance of oneself as a man, but the overwhelming urge occasionally to dress as and behave like a woman. (There are also female transvestites, but they are less frequently written about and commented upon, except when their transvestism is a prelude to transsexualism, probably because it is vastly more socially acceptable for a woman to dress as a man than it is for a man to dress as a woman. A female transvestite is, therefore, less of a deviant than a male transvestite.) Transvestites may achieve such proficiency in cross-dressing that people do not notice anything strange when they pass them dressed as women.

Transsexuals tend to be homosexual in so far as they tend to prefer sexual contacts with a member of the sex to which they belong physically. Since they believe themselves to be people trapped in an anatomically wrong body, this desire is not subjectively experienced as homosexuality, but as heterosexuality, and consequently, a male-to-female transsexual is likely to prefer a man who is not a self-defined homosexual and a female-to-male transsexual is likely to prefer a woman who is not a self-defined lesbian as sexual partners.

This is a brief description of the background information on sex change operations and related phenomena, such as transvestism. What is so very interesting in these phenomena is the underlying overwhelming sexual dimorphism that becomes obvious when reading the literature. My major thesis here is that transsexual patients have an excessively narrow image of what constitutes 'sex-appropriate' behaviour, which is reflected in the attitudes of the attending clinicians (psychologists, therapists and medical doctors) and the family of origin of the patient. Were the notions of masculinity and femininity less rigid, sex change operations should be unnecessary. Rather than identify somebody with a 'gender identity problem' as sick, we could define a society which insists on raising boys and girls in a clearly differentiated manner as sick. What should be treated as a *social* pathology is treated as if it were normal and when it manifests its effect in individuals it is treated as an *individual* pathology, and is 'corrected', rather than any attempts being made to combat the issue at its root: the oppressive (non-human) definition of sex roles, and the lack of recognition of intermediate sexes in Western society and, apparently, Westernised Eastern society, if one can make such a statement on the basis of a few isolated cases.

Sexual Dimorphism in Transsexuality

Masculinity-Femininity in the Transsexual Patient

Anatomically, contrary to the prevailing notion, the sexes are not 'opposites'. In many ways we are biologically similar; for example, both males and females have so-called male and female hormones, but the proportions are different for the sexes. Besides the external and internal accessory sexual organs all else is shared between the sexes, although the distributions are, statistically speaking, different.

As far as physical traits are concerned, it is possible to differentiate between different physical characteristics, for example, pitch of voice — at the statistical level — between males and females, but the difference is one of range rather than an absolute difference. As far as character traits are concerned (e.g. gentleness, dependence, emotionality for women, roughness, independence, and non-emotionality for men) we can identify sex stereotypes (as Bem has done for the construction of the BSRI) and we can observe statistical distributions which point toward differences in the distribution of behaviour traits (e.g. greater verbal ability of girls and greater physical aggressiveness of boys). All people encompass in themselves some elements that are stereotypically ascribed to the other sex, and most people seem not to worry about that. However, when we read the accounts of transvestites and transsexuals, we are struck by the very rigid and sharp distinction that is drawn between so-called feminine and masculine attributes, and, more significantly, by the perceived inappropriateness of engaging in behaviours that are seen as being fitting for the other sex.

Jan Morris (1975), for example, in her description of the years of her changeover from male to 'female', makes very clear statements as to what she expects a man and a woman to be. She notes that ' ... my own notion of the female principle was one of gentleness as against force, forgiveness rather than punishment, give more than take, helping more than leading' (p.12). ' ... though my body often yearned to give, to yield, to open itself, the machine was wrong' (p.24). Contrast this with her description of a journalist colleague while Jan was still James Morris.

> Though I never heard evil spoken of him by a living soul, still we were antipathetic from the start. 'How marvelous it must be,' I once remarked to him by way of small talk, *apropos* of his great height, 'to be able to command every room you enter.' 'I do not want,' he replied in his most reproving liberal style, 'to command anything at all' — an unfortunate response, though he could not know it, *to one whose ideals of manhood had been molded by military patterns, and who liked a man to be in charge of things.* (p.75, second emphasis added)

Rather, therefore, than permit it to be legitimate for a man to be gentle, give rather than take, help rather than lead or command, Morris perceives of these character traits as only legitimate for a woman (instead of clearly human) — these yearnings that he himself had, were, therefore, for himself illegitimate. He accepts a sexual dimorphism which strictly separates the sexes in terms of character traits, thus trying to live up to an inhuman masculine image, which, after a while, proves to be too much for him. A similar picture emerges from other descriptions (e.g. in Meyer, 1974) and is particularly obvious, also, in transvestites.

In one transvestite club which has recently been studied, the men come for one evening a week to dress up as females, and they go, crossdressed, to outings. Typically, a man would have selected a female name for himself that would be used exclusively while he was dressed as a female, and that is referred to as his 'sister'. For reasons of keeping their everyday identity secret, only first names are used, and members would know each other by both names, the 'brother' and 'sister' names. If a person did not bring his suitcase with clothes, he might say that he did not bring his sister along, but that he might do so next week. Reading the accounts of these transvestites who appear in ultra-feminine apparel, with make-up, typically feminine clothes (rather than, for instance, blue jeans and a shirt), wigs, nylons, etc., it becomes apparent that they uphold a likewise ultra-masculine appearance when they are not 'dressed' (as females). Feinbloom (1976, p.126) comments:

> These men are visually perfect examples of 'compartmentalized' deviance. For the most part, their cross-dressing is carefully de-limited in time and place and hidden from the rest of their lives. Their appearance, occupations, avocations, etc., outside their dressing, are strictly masculine. For example, most are balding or keep their hair very short. They dress conservatively and appropriately. They walk and talk in a masculine way, from the way they cross their legs to the way they hold their cigarettes. Their jobs and hobbies are 'accounts' insofar as they are frequently very 'masculine' in quality. The reinforced message, as I said before, is that any man who races sportscars, parachute jumps, looks so much like a man, is an army sergeant or a top-level computer analyst could not possibly be a 'pansy' or a 'deviant'.

If it were personally and socially acceptable for these men to wear clothes with ruffles, bright colours and soft materials (as was, for instance, customary in the Middle Ages) and to show their softer and gentler and more dependent side in everyday life, it is an open question whether they would still feel the need to assume, temporarily but regularly, the outer appearance of a member of the other sex.

Sexual Dimorphism in the Family of Origin of Transsexuals

The etiology of transsexualism has not been determined. The only thing that seems clear is that social factors play an extremely important role, and that biological factors are, at the very most, contributing towards predisposing a person to become a transsexual, and that possibly they play no role at all. Stoller (1972) suggests the following factors when trying to give a first approximation of the etiology of female (i.e. female-to-male) transsexuals:

... (1) an infant who does not strike the parents at birth or later as beautiful, graceful, or 'feminine' (whatever that would be to parents of a newborn); (2) an infant who is not cuddly when held but who habitually pushes away, even if a good feeder; (3) a feminine mother who at the birth of this daughter and at times later in childhood is removed in affect from her child, most often by overt, severe emotional illness, usually depression; (4) a masculine father who is nonetheless not present psychologically in at least two crucial areas: (a) he does not support his wife in her depression and (b) he does not encourage this daughter's femininity in the ways fathers of feminine daughters do. Given these factors, the little girl is (5) shot into the breach that the father abandoned, the role of succoring husband; the motive that propels the drive toward masculinity seems to be the family's manufacturing out of this daughter a substitute male (a husband) to assuage ('treat') mother's depression. This is done by constant encouragement of masculinity by both parents. Simultaneously, the child on her own is inventing a role — the masculine father-substitute — to mitigate her own terrible loneliness by having a mother whom she cannot reach and who does not reach out to her. Soon the process becomes self-perpetuating, when what at first was the development of isolated areas of high performance that are not inherently masculine or feminine (e.g., throwing a ball well, not crying when hurt, facility with a tool) coalesce into an identity, a sense of masculinity. This occurs both by the family's invariably encouraging masculine behavior and by this masculine-oriented father's enjoying sharing masculine interests with his daughter (identification). (Stoller, 1972, p.50)

Whether or not these factors will, in future, really turn out to be the determining factors for generating female-to-male transsexualism, it is obvious that so far the only explanations that have some semblance of plausibility have been explanations which draw exclusively on social factors. One could speculate whether, if all the factors, as outlined by Stoller, were present in a family but if, in addition, there was a feeling transmitted that females can have all the interests that are usually identified as masculine, that females can be supportive of their mother, etc., there would still be a need on the part of the patient to visualise herself as male rather than female.

Bentler (1976) has recently attempted to isolate the possible developmental basis of male (male-to-female) transsexualism. Of 22 possible causes for male transsexualism which he enumerates, two are clearly biological in character (prenatal feminisation of the brain and inborn temperament to fussiness and unresponsiveness), one may be either biological or socially determined (low activity and energy level) and the rest are all social variables (presence of weak and non-nurturant father, learning of negative attitudes toward sexual organs, absence of consistent, effective rewards for sex role stereotyped behaviours and interests, learning not to look at females as sex objects, perceived difficulties with masculine work roles, development of a self-concept as different from other boys, etc.).

Clearly, possible explanations of transsexualism are at an early stage. Just as clearly, if people would delineate less sharply between males and females than they do at present, many of the suspected causes would simply cease to exist. The desire to be a member of the opposite sex presupposes very clear and mutually exclusive notions as to what each sex is like.

It is impressive to read some of the accounts of the manner in which parents distinguish between what is proper for a boy and what is proper for a girl. In one reported instance a family had two male-to-female transsexuals. During one of the interviews, the mother was asked:

Dr S: When you would buy them gifts for Christmas or birthdays, what would you get them when they were 2 or 3 years old?
Mother: I liked to buy them dolls. I like dolls. You know, *dressing* dolls I like. But I buy a little car.
T: Oh yeah. She used to buy us cars. She said she liked dolls. She wanted to buy us dolls but she bought us cars.
Dr S: Where did you get the dolls from?
T: My cousin's.
Dr S: When they were little, you would buy them boys' toys?
Mother: Yes. Sometimes they would play, but they would play with dolls. They like to play with dolls, and I say, 'NO!' (Stoller and Baker, 1973, p.327, emphases in the original)

On the other hand, it seems impossible at this point of time to weigh the familial influences against other social pressures. Since these transsexuals are from a culture which is highly sex-stereotyped and very conscious of 'sex-appropriate' behaviour, some children who had yearnings to behave in a 'sex-inappropriate' manner may have simply found it impossible to overcome the feeling of inappropriateness, and may have thereby been pushed to imagine themselves as members of the other sex who happen to be endowed with the wrong body.

Whatever the role of the family may be, one thing seems certain: clinicians who are attending transsexuals need to believe strongly in 'gender differentiation' in order to be willing to offer their services to transsexuals who request them.

Sexual Dimorphism in Attending Clinicians

The prevailing clinical view of transsexuals, transvestites and homosexuals is that they have a gender identity problem, that they have chosen improper sex objects (homosexuality) and that they behave, in a general way, in a gender-inappropriate manner. Indeed, a diagnosis of a gender identity problem is a prerequisite for obtaining sex reassignment surgery. The factor on which surgery seems to hinge is whether or not the patient is judged to have a primary identification as a member of the opposite sex.

It warrants a moment's reflection that the reason for which sex reassignment surgery is performed is gender confusion, and not sex confusion. In other words, the patients are all clearly aware what their anatomical sex is. There is absolutely no 'confusion' on this issue. The only 'confusion' is their refusal to behave in the manner that is socially prescribed for their sex.

Clinicians need to believe fairly strongly in the appropriateness of 'sex-appropriate behavior' and a 'proper gender identity' in order to be able to justify, to themselves and others, the removal of physiologically perfectly normal and healthy sex organs in substantial numbers of patients. Clinicians involved with transsexuals — at least those who perform sex reassignment surgery — must not only accept the present sex structure, but must passionately believe in its essential rightness.

There are different ways in which accounts can be read. So far, we have used accounts of transsexuals in order to extract information about the femininity-masculinity attitudes of the patients and their families. However, the same reports (when written by clinicians) can be used to extract not the problems of the patients, but the prejudices of clinicians. One example is particularly striking which is reported by Money, since it reveals at least as much about the clinician's concern with sex role behaviour and gender identity (and the malleability of the human character) as about any problems that the patient may have. It is especially interesting to examine this example because Money is one of the earliest authors who previously had advanced the thesis that humans are psychosexually undifferentiated at birth (Money, 1963, p.39). According to Money, Hampson and Hampson (1955, p.316) '...sexuality is undifferentiated at birth and...becomes differentiated as masculine or feminine in the course of the various experiences of growing up'. These conclusions are based on studies of people with inconsistent sex attributes (hermaphrodites) and, in general, the investigators found that infants can be successfully raised — irrespective of their biological sex — in either sex. In this particular example, the raising of a genetic male as a female is reported.

The case is one of identical male twin brothers, one of whom lost his penis through an accident at the age of seven months. Consequently, Money advised the parents to raise this child as a female:

> I gave them advice and counseling on the future prognosis and management of their new daughter, based on experiences with similar reassignments in hermaphroditic babies. In particular, they were given confidence that their child can be expected to differentiate a female gender identity, in agreement with her sex of rearing. (Money, 1975, p.67)

By the age of nine years (the age when this case was reported), the two identical (genetically male) twins showed two clearly differentiated personalities, with different dress preferences, different attitudes towards cleanliness, very different toy preferences, different duties around the house which were willingly performed, and generally a sharply differentiated behaviour structure. Money is very laudatory of the successful efforts of the mother to raise this child as a girl, and reports in positive terms on the mother's activities in these regards, e.g. 'in pointing out the specifics of the female and male adult reproductive roles', and 'their other different roles, such as wife and husband or financial supporter of the family and caretaker of children and house' (p.69).

> Regarding domestic activities, such as work in the kitchen and house traditionally seen as part of the female's role, the mother reported that her daughter copies her in trying to help her tidying and cleaning up the kitchen, while the boy could not care less about it. She encourages her daughter when she helps her in the housework. (Money, 1975, pp.69-70)

Through systematically applying a double standard (by differentially rewarding identical behaviour — e.g. the mother encourages the daughter when she helps her in the housework, but presumably she does not encourage the son) and with the expert guidance of the clinician two different sex identities of anatomically identical people are constructed. The result of the process is likely to be two more adults who will consider it fitting for the 'nature' of a woman to take care of house and children, and fitting for the 'nature' of a man to be the breadwinner of a family. The assisting clinician obviously perceives this as the appropriate role divison, and actively furthers this outcome. Considering that the girl is anatomically a boy, this case graphically illustrates — perhaps clearer than other cases of transsexualism, because we are here dealing with an involuntary transsexual — the completely arbitrary nature of our sex identity which is thereby shown not to be related to the presence of internal and/or external sex organs, counter to the claims of many psychologists.

In another study, Green (1976) compares 60 boys characterised by 'extensive cross-gender behaviour' who are seen as potential future transsexuals, and therefore of a pathological inclination. They were so identified if on a 'never, occasionally, or frequently trichotomy' they 'at least occasionally cross-dressed, role-played as a female, preferred girls' toys and games, related better to girls, avoided rough-and-tumble play, and were called "sissy" by their peer group'. Instead of viewing a situation in which games are rigidly divided by sex, in which boys and girls are supposed not to like to play with each other, etc., as a case of social pathology, children who refuse to participate in this form of social sickness are seen as being individually pathological. It is striking that the discussion of transsexual pathology concerns almost exclusively gender identity rather than sex identity. Patients do not have a confused image about their sexual organs, although they display a strongly negative view of their own sex organs since these symbolise to them at the anatomical level the restrictions that they think they must accept at the personality level. Clinicians further this interpretation by themselves subscribing to a sexual dimorphism at the psychic level.

An alternative route would be not to attempt to convince these people to behave in a 'gender-appropriate manner', but to try to get them to accept themselves as men or women, boys or girls who happen to have tastes that are similar to those of many (but not all) members of the other sex rather than to those of many (but not all) members of their own sex. Such an effort may possibly be too late for patients who seek sex reassignment surgery, and in that sense one cannot fault clinicians if they do not succeed in fostering a more positive self-image which includes an acceptance of one's sex organs without any attempt to conform to rigid sex roles. However, this does not alter the fact that individual transsexuals are casualties of an overly rigid sex role differentiation, and that clinicians who perform sex reassignment surgery help to maintain this overly rigid sexual dimorphism which is restrictive to every human being, whether female, male, or transsexual.

There is also some evidence of a scientific double standard on the part of clinicians, i.e. a differential interpretation of data according to the sex of the actor. Stoller and Baker (1973, p.326), for example, when discussing the background of a male-to-female transsexual, note that he took some pride in getting away from his overly protective mother. 'When she [previously he] left the house, it was not to express masculine independence but was simply a rebellion against her mother's demands for housekeeping and for just staying in the house.' The action reported upon is asexual, but the interpretation offered is sexual.

Sexual dimorphism implies that one does not socially accept the presence of persons who are neither unambiguously male nor female, although in nature such people do exist, and in previous times at least some limited recognition was accorded to them.

Eunuchs and Intersexes

Biological sex is determined in different ways: chromosomal sex, gonadal sex, internal accessory organs, external genital appearance. In addition, the assigned sex and gender role may be consistent or inconsistent with the other determinants of sex (Rosenberg and Sutton-Smith, 1972, p.31). In most people, all four biological determinants of sex and the assigned sex and rearing coincide, so that we have persons who are both in anatomy and in behaviour unambiguously male or female. However, sometimes the determinants of sex are inconsistent with each other, and then we have cases of hermaphrodism, or mixed sex. The occurrence of different types of hermaphrodism has been estimated to be: for true hermaphrodites (with both male and female sex organs) very rare, for pseudomales 1 out of every 2,000, for pseudofemales also 1 out of every 2,000, for male pseudohermaphrodites 1 out of every 2,000, and for female pseudohermaphrodites 1 out of every 50,000 (*Encyclopedia Britannica*, 1973, vol. 11, p.432). Inconsistent sex therefore, is in any given population not a very frequent phenomenon; but at a world level, it is not an uncommon condition, either. In Western societies we regard these people with inconsistent sex variables as abnormal and we attempt to rear them unambiguously as either male or female, although this is inconsistent with their true 'intersex', since contemporary Western society has no social category for intersexes.

This has not always been the case. In some primitive societies, we find a social category for people who are neither female nor male but something else, for example, men who behave like women, or women who behave like men, etc. (Other primitive societies, however, would kill infants if they seemed somehow 'abnormal'.) A fair bit has been written about people with an intersex status (for a discussion, see Martin and Voorhies, 1975, pp.84-107), especially about the berdache, but Stoller (1976, pp.537-8) suggests that

> Although the subject has caught the attention of anthropologists and psychiatrists, this may be more for its oddity than frequency. Reviewing the anthropological literature, one cannot judge how many people like this existed at any time. My impression is that it was rare, so much so that whenever an anthropologist heard of such a person, a report was filed. The whole subject is mushy. And now it is too late to know.

Whatever the frequency — or rarity — of social intersexes may have been, it seems certain that quite a number of peoples recognise more than two sexes, and that these cultures were not threatened by men who wanted to live like women and women who wanted to live like men. For instance, Evans-Pritchard (1945) describes the case of Nyaluthni, a woman among the Nuer (a semi-nomadic nilotic tribe) who was rich and barren and purchased for herself two wives. The wives bore her two children by Dinka men who did not live in Nyaluthni's homestead but frequently visited it, stayed there for one or several nights, and hoed her gardens. She chose them as the genitors of her children because they were known to be hard-working gardeners. Her children

> address her as *gwa*, 'father', and not as *ma*, 'mother'. She is a woman of outstanding character, with fine features, and always well-dressed. She is very competent and runs her homestead like a man. If her wives are lazy or disobedient she beats them. They treat her with the respect due to a husband and place meals before her with the same ceremony as they would employ to a male husband. She speaks of them as 'my wives'. She directs the business of the Kraal and homestead with the skill of an experienced herdsman and householder and stands no interference in matters pertaining to cattle, even from her initiated son. (Evans-Pritchard, 1945, pp.31-2).

This is the case of a woman who has been socially defined as a man. There are two contemporary reported instances in which non-operative transsexuals are apparently fully accepted within their own culture: among contemporary American Indians and in Vietnam. In spite of being socially accepted within their own culture, these people expressed the wish for sex reassignment surgery, which is probably due to the influence of Westernised America on their own culture.

In the first of these instances, Stoller (1976) reports of two contemporary male Indians who desired surgery. Neither one reported any ridicule from his peers or parents for his propensity to live as a female, and at least one of them had obtained a very high status within his tribe as the best basketweaver and dressmaker of the tribe. The other case is about 'Mimi', another male-to-female (non-operative) transsexual in Vietnam. Mimi had been arrested as a prostitute by the police and was discovered to be a man only at the time of the routine gynaecological examination, at which point he was suspected to be a draft dodger and was sent to the army induction centre. He wanted to go to the United States for a sex change operation, but was apparently doing well in Vietnam as he was, and seemed to be relatively well-to-do. The authors reporting on this latter case distinguish between three distinct cultural attitudes towards transsexuals in contemporary Vietnam:

> First, it provides an institutionalized transsexual role with high status and power in the society, perhaps in some ways similar to the Koniag culture and the Chuckchee shaman. Second, there is a tolerant attitude with low prestige but not social ostracism, perhaps similar to the Zuni 'la-mana'. This tolerance is extended to prepubertal children but appears to be considerably less for adults. Finally, westernized Vietnam appears similar to the United States in its strong societal disapproval of the marginal role for the transsexual. (Heiman and Le, 1975, pp.93-4)

Not only does Western society not award an official — and even less a high and powerful — status to people who behave in a 'sex-inappropriate' manner, we also socially deny the existence of people who — since birth or later in life — have changed in some aspect of their sexuality, such as through castration. It used to be the case that in a number of societies, being a eunuch (castrated male) was a recognised sexual status, which was often combined with a powerful political status. Eunuchs tended to be considered as good political advisers, since they were thought to be more likely to be loyal to the ruling dynasty because of their incapacity to sire children. Accordingly, eunuchs were used as political advisers in a number of empires, such as in China during the Chou period, and under the Han, T'ang, Ming and Sung emperors. The Achaeminid Persians employed political eunuchs, as did some Roman emperors and most of the emperors of Byzantium. Many of the patriarchs of Constantinople were eunuchs (*Encyclopedia Britannica*, 1973, vol. 8, p.822). The Italians used to castrate boys in order to train them as adult sopranos. Without wishing to suggest that it is a recommendable practice to castrate boys (for whatever reason), I simply wish to point out that castrated males were in the past socially recognised as castrated males, whereas today they are likely to be treated as females, as was the twin who lost his penis as reported by Money (1975).

As a little side observation, it is interesting to note that while we have a historical name for castrated males (namely eunuch) we have no corresponding name for castrated females (women with hysterectomies), possibly because the changes in appearance are not as observable.

The Last Bulwark of the Double Standard

At present, the prevailing sex roles are under attack. At the social level, this manifests itself in collective movements, such as the women's liberation movement and the total woman movement as a backlash, the men's liberation movement and the National Organization for Men as a backlash, the gay liberation movement and the anti-homosexual movement (in the United States spearheaded by Anita Bryant) as a backlash. At the individual level, this is likely to result in more problems for some individuals who feel threatened by the gradual change in sex roles that is occurring. For others, it opens up options which have not been previously available to the same degree. Although changes in sex roles tend to be discussed in terms of female liberation, a change in the role of one sex necessitates a change in the role of the other. Widening of options — for members of both sexes — is as frightening to some as it is exhilarating to others.

While sex roles have been increasingly under attack, sex change operations have also become increasingly popular during the past few years. Historical reviews (e.g., Pauly, 1974a and 1974b, and Bullough, 1975) report only sparse information on older transsexuals. According to Pauly (1974b, p.520) the 'legitimization of sex reassignment surgery is vastly superior to that which existed only a few years ago'. The increase in numbers and medical legitimisation of sex reassignment surgery is partially a reflection of the increase in technological expertise for performing such operations, and the fact that only when the availability of such operations is known will people request it. On the other hand, sex change operations seem to have achieved some modicum of respectability which would indicate a change in the attitudes among physicians.

From a strictly physiological viewpoint, we must designate sex change operations as bodily mutilation — the wilful destruction of physically healthy portions of the body for purely social reasons. What is absolutely stunning to me is the fact that, when asked, transsexuals do not seek this form of bodily mutilation primarily for sexual reasons (which seems to me the only conceivable justification) but for social reasons, as the completion of a process of transformation into a member of the other sex. And yet, the transformation can never truly take place, even if phalloplasty and vaginoplasty were vastly improved.

In the follow-up study of 42 male-to-female post-operative transsexuals, the transsexuals were asked to rank nine possible alternatives for 'your basic motivations for getting your sex changed'. The primary reason that was given was 'to make my body more like my mind, as a woman', over such alternatives as the wearing of pretty clothing, being less aggressive, avoiding masculine expectations, having sex with a male, eliminating the male self through amputation of the penis, competing with another female, and winning the love of a parent. When the transsexuals were asked, after surgery, 'Which have you found to be more important and satisfying, your life as a female (able to have sex with males) or your social role as a woman in society?' the averages clearly showed that for the subjects surgery was important for non-sexual reasons (Bentler, 1976, p.569).

Seeking a sex change operation presupposes that the individual concerned considers him/herself incapable of achieving the goals that he or she has within the given body. This implies a mechanical identification of certain behaviour and character traits with one's anatomy which is so strong that people are willing to have their bodies mutilated in order to decrease the differential between their preferred behaviour and the restriction that they see as being set on this behaviour through their bodies. Performing the operation implies that the physicians agree that the perceived discrepancy is a real discrepancy — that indeed the behaviours and traits displayed are appropriate for a member of the other sex only. Patient and doctor thus jointly reinforce the idea that behaviour and character traits are legitimately determined by one's body, in the face of the evidence that suggests that our sex identity is imposed on a sexually largely or entirely undifferentiated character structure, and that, therefore, sex identity is a social rather than a biological product.

The rationale for sex reassignment surgery seems to be based on a circular logic which goes like this. Sex determines character. This is natural. Therefore, cases in which biological sex does not result in the expected sex identities are unnatural. Consequently, we need to change the biological sex (i.e. nature) in order to uphold the principle that biological sex determines one's character.

Transsexuals are people who suffer so deeply from the sex structure that they are willing to endure terrible pain and loneliness in order to reduce their suffering. This group of people would – potentially – be the most potent group of people pressing for changes in the sex structure, because their aversion to their 'sex-appropriate' roles is apparently insurmountable. By declaring them, by surgical fiat, as members of the other sex, this change potential is diverted and becomes as conservative as it could have been revolutionary. Each situation is individualised, rather than being recognised as the result of a social pathology, and the social pathology has overcome one more threat to its continued well-being.

Jan Morris (1975, p.192), who underwent sex reassignment surgery, addressed this issue as follows:

> Is mine only a transient phenomenon, between the dogmatism of the last century, when men were men and women were ladies, and the eclecticism of the next, when citizens will be free to live in the gender role they prefer? Will people read of our pilgrimage to Casablanca, a hundred years hence, as we might read of the search for the philosopher's Stone, or Simeon Stylites on his pillar?
>
> I hope so. For every transsexual who grasps that prize, identity, ten, perhaps a hundred discover it to be only a mirage in the end, so that their latter quandry is hardly less terrible than their first.

Once we recognise the social pathology which creates the discussed individual pathologies, we must recognise the call of clinicians such as Pauly's (1974b, p.522) that 'Parents ought to be more aware of the need to positively reinforce all infants for those gender characteristics which are consistent with their biological identity' as an attempt to ensure the continuing existence of the preconditions from which the problems with which these clinicians are concerned arise.

Notes

1. As noted in the introduction, many people distinguish between gender and sex, with sex referring to biological and gender to social differences between the sexes. Having tried for a while to use this terminology, I have since given it up as confusing. As a rule, I only use the term 'sex'. In this chapter, however, I shall use the term 'gender' when I am discussing authors who use the term.

2. I am suggesting that the scales have become ossified because there is a tendency to continue to use scales once they have been 'validated' for reasons of comparability.

3. In a more recent paper, Bem (1977) concurs with the suggestion that the BSRI ought to be scored so as to yield four rather than three distinct groups, namely masculine (high masculine, low feminine scores), feminine (high feminine, low masculine scores), androgynous (high masculine and low feminine scores) and undifferentiated (low masculine and low feminine scores). Although this introduces a variation into the operationalisation of androgyny, it does not alter the basic problem underlying androgyny scores.

References

Bem, Sandra L. 'The Measurement of Psychological Androgyny', *Journal of Clinical Psychology,* vol. 42, no. 2 (1974), pp.155-62.

Bem, Sandra L. 'On the Utility of Alternative Procedures for Assessing Psychological Androgyny', *Journal of Consulting and Clinical Psychology*, vol. 45, no. 2 (1977), pp.166-205.

Bentler, Peter M. 'A Typology of Transsexualism: Gender Identity Theory and Data', *Archives of Sexual Behavior*, vol. 5, no. 6 (1976), pp.567-83.

Bullough, Vern L. 'Transsexualism in History', *Archives of Sexual Behavior*, vol. 4, no. 5 (1975), pp.561-71.

Decision Marketing Research Ltd. *Women in Canada* (Ottawa, Office of the Coordinator, Status of Women, 2nd edn., 1976).

Eichler, Margrit, 'Power, Dependency, Love and the Sexual Division of Labour. A Critique of the Decision-Making Approach to Family Power and an Alternative Approach' (unpublished paper).

Encyclopedia Britannica, vol.s 8 and 11 (1973 edn.).

Evans-Pritchard, E.E. *Some Aspects of Marriage and the Family among the Nuer* (The Rhodes-Livingstone Papers no. 11) (Livingstone, Northern Rhodesia, The Rhodes Livingstone Institute, 1945).

Feinbloom, Deborah Heller. *Transvestites and Transsexuals* (USA, Delacorte Press/Seymour Lawrence, 1976).

Green, Richard, 'One-Hundred Ten Feminine and Masculine Boys: Behavioral Contrasts and Demographic Similarities', *Archives of Sexual Behavior*, vol. 5, no. 5 (1976), pp. 425-46.

Heiman, Elliott M. and Cao Van Le. 'Transsexualism in Vietnam', *Archives of Sexual Behavior*, vol. 4, no. 1 (1975), pp.89-95.

Holter, Harriet. *Sex Roles and Social Structure* (Oslo, Bergen, Tromso, Universitetsforlaget, 1970).

Hore, B.D., F.V. Nicolle and J.S. Calnan. 'Male Transsexualism: Two Cases in a Single Family', *Archives of Sexual Behavior*, pp.317-31.

Laurie, Bonnie. 'An Assessment of Sex-Role Learning in Kindergarten Children: Experimental Application of a Toy Test with Direct Reinforcement of Sex-

Typed and of Androgenous Behaviour' (unpublished MA thesis, Dept. of Educational Theory, University of Toronto, 1977).

Martin, M. Kay and Barbara Voorhies. *Female of the Species* (Toronto, Methuen, 1975).

Meyer, Jon K. 'Clinical Variants Among Applicants for Sex Reassignment', *Archives of Sexual Behavior*, vol. 3, no. 6 (1974), pp.527-58.

Money, John. 'Development Differentiation of Femininity and Masculinity Compared', in *Man and Civilization: The Potential of Woman* (New York, McGraw-Hill, 1963), pp.51-65.

Money, John. 'Ablatio Penis: Normal Male Infant Sex-Reassigned as a Girl', *Archives of Sexual Behavior*, vol. 4, no. 1 (1975), pp.65-71.

Money, John and Anke A. Ehrhardt. *Man and Woman, Boy and Girl* (New York: New American Library, 1974).

Money, John, J.L. Hampson and J.G. Hampson, 'An Examination of some Basic Sexual Concepts: The Evidence of Human Hermaphroditism' *Bulletin of the Johns Hopkins Hospital*, vol. 97 (1955), pp.301-19.

Money, John and George Wolff. 'Sex Reassignment: Male to Female to Male', *Archives of Sexual Behavior*, vol. 2, no. 3, (1973), pp.245-50.

Morris, Jan. *Conundrum* (New York, Signet Books, 1975).

Pauly, Ira B. 'Female Transsexualism: Part 1', *Archives of Sexual Behavior*, vol. 3, no. 5 (1974a) pp.487-507.

Pauly, Ira B. 'Female Transsexualism: Part II', *Archives of Sexual Behavior*, vol. 3, no. 6 (1974b) pp.509-26.

Rosenberg, B.G. and Brian Sutton-Smith. *Sex and Identity* (New York, Holt, Rinehart and Winston, 1972).

Sawyer, Jack. 'On Male Liberation', in Deborah S. David and Robert Brannon (eds.), *The Forty-Nine Percent Majority: The Male Sex Role* (Reading, Mass., Addison-Wesley Publ. Co., 1976), pp. 287-90.

Stoller, Robert, 'Etiological Factors in Female Transsexualism: A First Approximation', *Archives of Sexual Behavior*, vol. 2, no. 1 (1972), pp.47-64.

Stoller, Robert J. 'Two Feminized Male American Indians', *Archives of Sexual Behavior*, vol. 5, no. 6 (1976) pp.529-38.

Stoller, Robert J. and Howard J. Baker. 'Two Male Transsexuals in One Family', *Archives of Sexual Behavior*, vol. 2, no. 4 (1973), pp.323-8.

Swift, Jonathan. *Gulliver's Travels* (New York, Airmont Books, 1963).

4 THE DOUBLE STANDARD IN THE SOCIAL STRUCTURE: THE INADEQUACY OF CLASS ANALYSIS

Today, hardly anyone would dispute that sex stratification exists. What is being disputed is (a) how exactly the sex differences in power, authority, prestige, economic wealth and social position manifest themselves and (b) how they can best be described and/or analysed. Which differences are of primary importance, which ones of secondary or tertiary importance? The answers to these questions are not only important for their own sakes, but have implications for the self-understanding of women and men. Depending on how the emphases are placed, different political strategies seem appropriate for changing or preserving, according to one's stance towards sex equality, the social sex structure. In other words, we cannot elaborate a strategy for change unless we have first correctly identified the bases and major manifestations of sex stratification. A critique and evaluation of different approaches to the stratification of the sexes is, therefore, a necessary prerequisite for critical assessment of strategies for change.

Within the literature that deals with sex stratification we can distinguish four basically different approaches. In ascending order of sociological importance, we can identify them as:
1. theories of biological sex status;
2. theories of women and men as status groups;
3. multivariate approaches to sex stratification; and
4. class analysis.

Each of these major approaches can be subdivided into several further categories. Theories of biological sex status, for instance, can be subdivided into theories which maintain that women are superior, inferior, or different but equal to men. Theories of women and men as status groups can be subdivided into attempts to comprehend women as a minority group or as a caste. In addition, some of the attempts to analyse women as a class can be understood as a sub-variant of the general theoretical postulate that women and men form status groups. In this chapter, however, we will not consider the postulate that women form a class under the heading of women and men as status groups, because the analysis of women as a class needs to be placed into the context of over-all class analysis. Multivariate approaches differ in the number and type of variables included. Class analysis, finally, has been applied in two major ways to sex stratification: first, in attempts to comprehend women as a class and second, in attempts to analyse the importance of sex in a class-based society.

In this chapter, we shall deal with all four approaches — the first three briefly, and the fourth in greater detail because of its eminent sociological significance.

Theories of Biological Sex Status

According to this school of thought, women are permanently inferior, superior, or 'different but equal' to men because of their biological sex. Any social stratification based on sex is, therefore, merely the social consequence of a biological difference.

It is irrelevant for the understanding of this approach whether the claim made is that women are inferior, superior, or different but equal, since it is strictly a matter of power who decrees what is a criterion of inferiority, superiority, or essential equivalence. There seems to be little doubt that women are superior to men in strictly biological terms if this can be measured by a longer life expectancy and immunity to certain diseases, or rather a greater susceptibility of males towards a number of physical afflictions. However, since this biological superiority (if one wishes to use that term) is not only not reflected in social reality but tends to be inversely related to it, this presumed biological superiority is irrelevant in our context which concerns itself with social stratification.

To conceive of sex status in raw biological terms implies that there are only two strata — women and men — which may, each of them, be internally stratified, but which are always in some determinate manner related to each other. Since the stratification (whether it be sub- or superordination) is seen to generate directly from a biological difference, it is not seen as susceptible to change. Basically, after the relationship of women and men as groups has been identified in some manner, one cannot apply the same criteria to both, since men and women are fundamentally different. In other words, male values cannot be understood as normative standards for women.

On this last point, some radical feminists and radical conservatives meet. They both agree that male and female are fundamentally different and that therefore they may need to be judged by differential standards. Erikson (1964, p.26), for example, writes:

> Since a woman is never not-a-woman, she can see her long-range goals only in those modes of activity which include and integrate her

natural dispositions. An emancipated woman thus does not necessarily accept comparisons with more 'active' male proclivities as a measure of her equivalence, even if and after it has become quite clear that she can match man's performance and competence in most spheres of achievement. True equality can only mean the right to be uniquely creative.

Some feminists would argue that 'the female principle' needs greater recognition, and needs to be valued more highly, but this again assumes that we can, in fact, identify a biologically based male or female principle.

The most fundamental characteristic of this approach is that it is non- or pre-sociological, for it assumes a direct relationship between a biological and a social difference. To attempt to alter the essential sex difference would be futile, and effort for changes must therefore be geared towards a change in the evaluation of each of the sex statuses. This argument overlooks the fact that social evaluation is a function of social position and that, consequently, efforts to upgrade an evaluation without a corresponding change in position are doomed to failure.[1]

The most sophisticated version of biological stratification theory is found in Collins (1972), since it presents itself not as a biological approach but as a sociological approach. According to Collins (1972, p.58), the basis of sex stratification, which expresses itself in male dominance at home and at work, is

(1) that human beings have strong sexual and aggressive drives; and (2) that males are physically dominant over females, since they are generally bigger, and females are further made physically vulnerable by bearing and caring for children. The combination of these propositions means that men will generally be the sexual aggressors, and women will be sexual prizes for men.

This results in an element of coercion that is 'thus potentially present in every sexual encounter, and this shapes the fundamental features of the woman's role' (Collins, 1972, p.59).

Variations in sexual stratification are then explained through four ideal types of social structure which have differential male and female resources, which each result in a distinct system of sexual roles and a dominant sexual ideology. Collins thus tries to explain different forms of sex stratification in terms of different social structures and differential resources for women and men. However, it remains unclear what the connection is between the basic pattern of male sexual ownership of women and the variations introduced through the social structure. The over-all impression is that through increased resources women have increased their bargaining power which has resulted in an equalisation of the position of the sexes, and that any inequalities that remain are due to the basic biological difference as cited above. Basically, then, sexual inequality (= sex stratification) is explained in terms of a biological difference, but decreases in inequality are explained through social factors. In other words, we continue to explain social facts (sex stratification) through biological facts (male physical dominance due to larger male size and female childbearing capacity). Any sex stratification existing today in advanced market economies is essentially seen as a residual effect of a biological difference.

Theories of Women and Men as Status Groups

The concept of women and men as status groups is expressed in two other forms besides that which interprets women as a class, one using 'women as a minority group' and the other 'women as a caste'. This indicates the first general problem with this approach: the concept of minority group only makes sense in the context of a dominant (or majority) group, and the concept of caste only makes sense in the context of a caste system, i.e. a minimum of two hierarchically ordered castes. To discuss the concepts of minority group and caste we should therefore speak of 'women as a minority group and men as dominant group' and 'women and men as castes'. The fact that this is usually not done suggests that the position of men is seen as unproblematic.

Women as Minority Group and Men as Dominant Group

The designation of women as a minority group is by no means recent. Hacker (1951) first elaborated the concept and, since that time, little has been added to it. Since Hacker's article has been widely reprinted and cited recently, a short criticism seems in place.

In its substance, the article is still depressingly appropriate and timely, even to a comment on the non-ratification of the Equal Rights Amendment in the USA. In terms of an analysis of sex stratification, Hacker argues that women display many of the psychological attributes of a minority group, such as group self-hatred, a person's tendency to denigrate other members of the group, acceptance of the dominant group's stereotypes, and attempts to distance oneself from the group. She also adds that the majority of women are in all likelihood not displaying a minority group consciousness. This latter statement is probably no longer correct due to the influence of the Women's Liberation Movement. Today, many women do feel discriminated against.

If women are a minority group, men should be the dominant group. This latter factor is left unanalysed, as often happens in minority group analysis, since it is the status of the minority group that is seen as problematic and not that of the majority group.

The analogy between women and minority groups is clearly useful for focusing on the psychic mechanisms in inter-sexual interactions, and it is, even today, suggestive and stimulating. However, as a stratification concept, it is very limited: it focuses solely on the consequences of belonging to a minority group but does not tell us anything about the power relationship as such, its variations, limitations, different manifestations, etc. It contrasts men and women as two groups, thus drawing our attention to the differences *between* the groups without at the same time considering the differences *within* each of the two groups. Are within-group power differences significantly smaller than between-group differences? Are they as great? Or greater? If the within-group differences are as great or greater than those between the two groups, how meaningful is it to continue to utilise the concept of minority group for women?

For instance, one could argue that old and/or young people (children) constitute minority groups. Both the old and the young have to live in a culture which is not geared to their needs, they are discriminated against in many ways — economically, socially, politically (the young are entirely politically disenfranchised, and the old are often *de facto* politically disenfranchised), they are spatially segregated (children can be sent out of adult areas in private homes as well as in public spaces, and the old are segregated into old-age homes of various kinds), there is social distance between the young and the 'adult' population which is not yet the 'old' population, and between the 'old' population and the 'adult' population; each group has a culture of its own, etc.

The point is not to elaborate on the concept of various age groups as minority groups, but to ask what happens when we introduce other stratifying variables into the equation. Clearly, there are stratifying variables other than sex (e.g. age, riches, etc.). However, the analysis does not lend itself to further refinement, the notion of a minority group within a minority group (or even further a minority group within a minority group within a minority group) is not practicable. The notion of women as a minority group is, although suggestive, not capable of any sort of refined analysis — nor was it intended to constitute a comprehensive theory of sex stratification when it was first applied to women.

Women and Men as Castes

Castes can be described as groups of people which make up hereditary, birth-ascribed, endogamous subdivisions in a hierarchy. A rigid distinction leads to distinct cultures, and the hierarchy entails differential evaluation, differential reward and differential association (Berreman, 1968, pp.333-9).

Clearly, men and women are not castes in the strict sense of the word. One of the most important characteristics of caste is endogamy, while women and men constantly intermarry — indeed, homosexual marriages are illegal in most countries. Likewise, it is clearly too simplistic to picture women and men as two strata which are in a strictly hierarchical relationship, with the men on the top and the women at the bottom. We know that there are many women whose rank — by whatever criterion — is higher than that of many men. Further, although there are indications of distinct female and male cultures, there is also a widely shared culture between the sexes, and there are shared cultural subdivisions along lines other than sex, such as economic positions, ethnicity, religion, urban-rural distinctions, etc.

However, most researchers who use the concept of women and men as castes do not mean such a literal translation. Myrdal (1944), who was the first writer to popularise the notion of women as a caste, says explicitly in his famous Appendix 5 to 'An American Dilemma' that he is drawing a parallel. He is making an analogy, not suggesting a rigid transference of caste relationships to sex relationships. Many people would currently acknowledge this loose fit between the concept of caste and the position of the sexes by referring to women as possessing a 'caste-like status' (e.g. Ambert, 1976, p.191 and Glazer-Malbin, 1976). This concept indicates that within given strata (such as classes) women occupy a lower position by virtue of their sex and that there are certain characteristics that women share because of their sex which are birth-ascribed, which result in a differential evaluation from men, in differential rewards and differential association. Used in this manner, describing the sexes as castes is not an attempt to map exhaustively the power relationships of the sexes, but to focus attention on sex status as a contributing factor in a stratification system. This is certainly an unobjectionable statement, but the concept is misleading, as it is only half-applicable. Identifying sex as a stratification variable conveys the same message in a clearer manner. The notion of women and men as castes, in other words, does not add any information that could not be expressed more clearly without the help of this concept.

Multivariate Approaches to Sex Stratification

By far the most popular approach to sex stratification in the social sciences is the multivariate approach. Here, society is understood as stratified along various dimensions, e.g. education, income, occupation, age, ethnicity, religion, authority, and others. What and how many dimensions are being considered varies by author. Sex is seen as one variable among others in this stratification model which functions to depress the status of women in society, all other things being equal (meaning the rankings in all other relevant dimensions).

Since the multivariate approach is probably the dominant approach to social stratification at the present time in North America, it is not surprising that people concerned with sex stratification have attempted to integrate sex as one other stratifying variable into the already existing model of stratification. Further, the integration is not too difficult to achieve. Lastly, this type of approach lends itself to detailed sophisticated statistical analysis, and is generally seen as the appropriate method for interpreting survey data. This approach is sometimes equated with one form of class analysis.

The cumulative findings of the work that has gone into this approach can be summarised as follows: no matter what the other status variables, female sex tends to depress the over-all status of a person. This general tendency has been observed in many specific ways: women with equivalent educational characteristics have lower-placed jobs than men. Women with equivalent types of jobs earn less money than men. Women with equivalent credentials are less well accepted in positions of authority. Etc.

These studies have added important new types of information to our knowledge about the effect of sex structure. The inclusion of sex into multivariate stratification models has made obvious what was not universally accepted before: that sex does, indeed, have an effect on social stratification that is independent of all other variables. So far, so good.

As a theory of sex stratification *per se*, however, multivariate analysis as presently conceived is unusable, not for any intrinsic methodological reasons, but because of the historical fact that, as in caste and minority group analysis, the inclusion of sex as a variable, and of women as a group, was an afterthought. The models were first constructed with only men in mind. Consequently, such factors as are important to explain why one man has more power, influence or prestige than some other man make up the variables in the stratification model.

When we measure status and mobility, we consider such variables as income (meaning primarily earned income from one's job), occupational prestige (which has so far excluded housewifery as an occupation) and education (meaning formal education). Mobility has been traditionally measured by comparing a male individual's ranking with that of his father, or a female's husband's ranking with that of her father. Women, in other words, have historically been seen in terms of their father's or husband's social standing. While for women with a paid job the model can be adapted, it remains inapplicable for housewives. Attempts to measure the occupational prestige of housewives have been made (Bose, 1976 and Eichler, 1977), with results which are quantifiable and could be integrated into the computation of social status. However, this means that we accept that occupational prestige is, indeed, a stratification variable which indicates the salient aspects of a woman's position in the social system. I would submit that this assumption is unwarranted.

Occupational prestige is a depersonalised variable, while the occupation of housewifery draws its social rewards from personal contacts. It may be far more important for the housewife what her immediate family, relatives, friends and neighbours think about her performance than what points she would gain on some occupational prestige scale. Besides, the prestige of a housewife varies quite considerably with her husband's occupation (Eichler, 1977). Most importantly, however, the occupation housewife is not a good predictor of other status variables, such as education. Women of all educational levels, of all races, ages, ethnic groups, and with husbands in all strata may be housewives. One general question, therefore, is whether occupations should continue to be accorded the important place they have been able to command in multivariate stratification models. A more basic question is whether multivariate approaches have so far been able to identify and incorporate into their model such variables as are of primary importance to women.

Let us reflect for a moment on the meaning of social stratification. Stratification models are supposed to identify and put into a context variables that result in social inequalities, and to predict the consequences of possessing certain status characteristics. On the basis of knowing how a man is located within a particular stratification system, we can predict with some accuracy the amount of power he has to control himself and others in relation to the amount of power held by differently placed men in the same social system. For instance, we know that the attitudes and behaviour of law-enforcing agencies are more deferential and less punitive towards people whom they perceive as having a high social standing than towards those whom they perceive to have a low social standing.

The relevant dimensions of power can be identified as control over one's own personal life, influence over community affairs, and influence over national affairs. One might also add influence over international affairs. The first of these variables, control over one's own personal life, is the one which touches people most immediately. For men there is generally a direct equation between social standing as customarily defined (type of occupation, level of education, level of income, and other variables) and personal autonomy, so that it may not be unreasonable to try to make judgements about their personal autonomy on the basis of the usual indicators. For women, however, the equation does not hold, because for women the family structure is critically important. Neither this factor, nor the fact that there is a complex social structure outside the family which maintains the prevailing inequality in the family, has ever yet been taken into consideration in a multivariate analysis of stratification.

In terms of work autonomy, housewifery may be very high, very low, or in between. Identifying a woman's occupation does not therefore necessarily allow us to predict the level of her work autonomy. More fundamental than work autonomy is the control over one's own well-being which includes freedom from threat of personal injury through familial violence.

For a long time it has been a well-guarded secret that there is a high level of intrafamilial violence, a great deal of which takes the form of wife beating. Only recently have researchers paid attention to this problem (e.g. Martin, 1976, Pizzey, 1974, Steinmetz and Straus, 1974, Whitehurst, 1977, Pleck 1977, Chan 1977, Steinmetz, 1978). Apparently, wife beating is a much more common occurrence than has previously been acknowledged, and references to 'the relatively peaceful middle-class' family structure (Collins, 1972, p.75) are hopelessly romantic fictions. Bell (1977) has demonstrated that most murders in Canada occur within the family. Although it is at this point impossible to make an accurate estimate of the over-all occurrence of wife beating, all evidence points to the fact that is by no means infrequent, and that it occurs in all social strata. Since freedom from the threat of violence against one's health and sometimes life is such a fundamental issue, any stratification approach which does not incorporate into the analysis such a basic variable does not adequately reflect the nature or extent of sexual inequality.

The basic problem with the multivariate approach to sex stratification is, therefore, that it remains a model that was devised with men in mind. It has been uneasily expanded to incorporate women along the dimensions important for men, but it does not yet deal with the extremely important issue of sexual inequality within the family.

Class Analysis

Marxists tend to think of themselves as the only radicals. By implication, Marxist feminists maintain that feminism cannot be radical unless it is placed within the context of class society and the oppression of women is understood within the basic politico-economic structure of the state, of which classes are one — albeit the most important — manifestation. Here I want to argue that as far as women and feminism are concerned, Marxist analysis is not only not radical but eminently conservative, in so far as its definition of social class is a completely androcentric definition in which women have no place except as objects that link men to men. Attempts to incorporate women into class analysis have been unsuccessful to date, inevitably so since the crucial concepts in class analysis are inapplicable to the situation of women.

Class analysis attempts to do two things: on the one hand, it raises questions concerning inequality, its causes, manifestations, and consequences; on the other hand, it allows us to pigeonhole people into a hierarchically ordered category system. It is irrelevant what precisely the terminology employed is — whether we talk about working class, lower class, upper class, middle class, ruling class, petty bourgeois class, etc. In all instances does class analysis provide a means for identifying people as members of a higher or lower class, whatever its name. On the basis of such a categorisation we then make statements about the relationship of the classes to each other.

Today, the first part of what class analysis attempts to do (examining inequality) remains as important as ever. It is in its second aspect that class analysis is no longer adequate. Although one might conceivably want to defend social classes as a system of categorisation that was at some time in history adequate, in present-day highly industrialised countries the categorisation system is no longer sufficient, since it is incapable of categorising women in a meaningful manner.

People who argue that questions of inequality are important rather than categorical aspects overlook the fact that we cannot possibly discuss relationships of groups with each other in an adequate manner if these groups have been improperly defined. The two aspects of class analysis are necessarily linked, and one cannot deal properly with the one if the other has been mishandled.

In the following, I shall attempt to demonstrate why class analysis misplaces women in its categorisation and why it must continue to do so in spite of the efforts of various analysts to incorporate women into the analytic framework. This does not imply that I question the existence or importance of social inequality and stratification, but that I consider the class model as no longer an adequate framework within which this discussion can be meaningfully carried out.

I shall use Ossowski's (1963) analysis of the class concept as a convenient starting-point, because he summarises different types of conceptions of social class, in the process comparing a Marxist with a non-Marxist definition of class. Ossowski distinguishes between two basic conceptions of social class, a broad and a narrow one. The broad concept of social class signifies any 'group which is regarded as one of the basic components of the social structure' (p.129). There are two specifying, narrower conceptions of social class, the first being 'a group distinguished in respect of the relations of property' or, in Marxian terms, a group that is distinguished according to its relation to the means of production. In the second specifying version of the concept of class, 'the class-concept is contrasted with group-systems in the social structure in which an individual's membership of a group is institutionally determined and in which privileges or discriminations result from an individual's ascription to a certain group' (p.130). Class membership is a consequence of achieved social status rather than being assigned (as a title of nobility would be) through birth certificate or an official document.

Having made the distinction between the broad and the two narrow conceptions of social class, Ossowski proceeds to elaborate three generally accepted assumptions relating to the concept of class and class society. These three shared assumptions are as follows:

1. The classes constitute a system of the most comprehensive groups in the social structure.
2. The class division concerns social statuses connected with a system of privileges and discriminations not determined by biological criteria.
3. The membership of individuals in a social class is relatively permanent. (p.133)

It is illuminating to note that the sole reason for including a biological criterion (in assumption no.2) is to exclude 'the privileges and discriminations assigned directly by sexual criteria,' (p.134). This restriction simply makes explicit the point we are trying to prove here, namely, that women are excluded from class analysis.

Ossowski then postulates four characteristics which are a consequence of the previously elaborated, but usually tacit assumptions elaborated above and which are inherent to all conceptions of social class. These are:

> 1. the vertical order of social classes: the existence of superior and inferior categories of social statuses, which are superior or inferior in respect to some system of privileges and discriminations. When one accepts such a criterion, 'class structure' means as much as 'class stratification'.
>
> 2. The second characteristic is the distinctness of permanent class interests (a 'class' society being regarded as a society that is divided into large groups with distinct, important and permanent interests). . . .
>
> 3. The third characteristic is class consciousness. . . . A 'class' society in this sense is a society in which the majority of active members possess a class consciousness, and this is reflected in their behaviour.
>
> 4. Finally, the fourth of these characteristics which can provide a basis for belief that a given society is a 'class' society is social isolation. . . . A society is a 'class' society in respect to this characteristic if there exist within it distinct barriers to social intercourse and if boundaries can be drawn by means of an analysis of interpersonal relations. (pp.135-6)

By postulating that classes are the basic components of a social structure and at the same time explicitly ruling out the possibility of taking sexual discrimination as a relevant criterion for a class, sex is defined as an irrelevant stratifying variable. Women must either be totally ignored, or else seen to belong to the same class to which the male they are seen as attached to belongs.

In fact, both these avenues have been the prevalent modes of (not) dealing with women until recently. This poses a dilemma. Social stratification on bases other than sex is real, but so is sex stratification. We can no longer pretend that sex stratification does not exist, nor that it exists but is unimportant.

There are two ways of approaching this dilemma. Ossowski's second assumption can be ruled out and women can be understood as a separate social class. Alternatively, one can attempt to adapt the crucial concepts in class analysis to accommodate women. I shall argue that either attempt is inconsistent with the internal logic of class analysis and that the only other avenue is either to continue to ignore women or else to declare class analysis as altogether inadequate.

Women as a Social Class

If we ignore the restriction contained in Ossowski's second assumption women can be conceived of as a social class in terms of his four characteristics of a social class. First, women and men are in a hierarchically ordered relationship in which men are superior with respect to a definite system of privileges and discriminations, for example in terms of access to high-prestige occupations, in terms of higher pay, in terms of access to positions of authority, etc. There are definite legal privileges and discriminations which are based on sex. Second, the distinction is relatively permanent, and has resulted in different interests for the sexes, for instance in issues concerning sexual relations such as rape laws (in which a male legal system seems to extend more protection to the male rapist than to the female rapee), in the division of property in marriages, and in the maintenance of women as a cheap and replaceable portion of the labour force. Thirdly, although we do not tend to think of sex identity as a form of class consciousness, it is possible to interpret it in such a manner. Sex identity is considered one of the building stones of our personality, so basic that its existence is taken for granted in every 'normal' person and that any deviation from it (e.g. a 'gender dysphoria syndrome') raises grave concerns for people who then feel they have to 'treat' the 'sex identity confusion'. Sex identity is reflected in our daily behaviours and its permanence is guaranteed through a system of sex roles. Lastly, the characteristic of social distance between the sexes needs some reflection. Normally, marriage is seen as evidence of lack of social distance, and physical intercourse is perceived of as the most intimate act possible between two people. Our marriage texts propound just that, and the major Christian religions have erected large theological edifices around this notion. However, it is possible to have sexual intercourse without any attendant social intercourse. The most extreme instance of this is rape. It is significant that in most countries husbands are legally incapable of raping their wives. In other words, because it occurs in a legally sanctioned context, physical intercourse is assumed to be expressive of social intimacy and to be indicative of emotional closeness, regardless of evidence that this is not necessarily the case. In fact, intercourse itself may run the gamut from being the most tender, joyful and intimate interaction to being a brutal assault. It is therefore not a good indicator for social proximity or distance.

Despite engaging in physical intercourse and sharing the same living quarters for part of their waking lives and a fair portion of their sleeping lives, the sexes are socially segregated, although less so now than previously, through occupational and political sex segregation, in leisure activities, etc. If we no longer make the assumption that physical intercourse is necessarily an indication of social intimacy (and that, instead, having a few drinks together, sharing one's work problems, going bowling, playing cards, or discussing one's sexual experiences rather than engaging in them are some of the real indicators of social intimacy), we could make a strong case that the sexes are in fact socially distant from each other.[2]

In terms of Ossowski's general criteria for social class, therefore, women could reasonably be understood as a social class. This type of analysis has been explicitly undertaken by Marxist theorists. In Marxist terms, the primary criterion for class membership is a specific type of relationship to the means of production. Benston (1969, p.16) argues that women are a social class in so far as women constitute 'that group of people who are responsible for the production of simple use-values in those activities associated with the home and family'. Since men do not carry responsibility for such production, but instead are responsible for the production of exchange values on the labour market, this puts men and women into two distinct sets of relationships to the means of production and therefore groups them into two distinct classes.

Benston then goes on to argue that the material basis for the inferior position of women lies in the fact that women as a group work outside the money economy. 'Their work is not worth money, is therefore valueless, is therefore not even real work' (p.16). In the sense that all women do housework, which is unpaid labour, regardless of their labour force status (i.e. regardless of whether they do, in addition, paid labour) and regardless of the income level and occupation of their husbands, all women belong to the same class.

If we take this position seriously, it leads to a curious paradox. Both in Marxist and in non-Marxist class analysis women can be understood as a social class. Classes only make sense within a class system. Therefore, women as a class are part of a system in which men constitute the other class(es). The whole point of class analysis, before women were considered, was that men belong to different classes. Therefore, what is the relationship between the female class and the different male classes?

In their relationship to women men constitute one class only, in so far as they are the beneficiaries of the unpaid labour of women. In relation to each other, men are stratified into different classes. To argue anything else would be patently absurd. On the other hand, to argue that women constitute one social class only that is always exploited by men in the same manner seems to me equally absurd, since there are some women who are the beneficiaries of the surplus value produced by men. At the same time, these same women may perform unpaid labour which is exploited by other men.

Therefore, it is not even correct to conceive of women as a class within a class, since the relationships between women and women, and between women and men of different strata, are widely diverse since the performance of housework is only one aspect of the entire set of relationships involved, although an extremely important one.

Basically, the problem is that class analysis is not able to incorporate family structure, and that sex relations and sex stratification cannot be adequately dealt with unless we discuss the family structure. The social position of a woman is to a high degree determined by the family structure in which she finds herself. Whether she lives in a female-headed, a male-headed or an acephalous family structure, whether there are dependent children or not, whether there is violence between family members or not, are basic determinants of a woman's lifestyle and position. Whether or not a woman has her own independent income is likely to be more important for her than the amount of money her husband earns. To what degree and in what way the surrounding society treats her as a family member rather than as an individual —e.g. by making credit unavailable to married women unless they have their husband's consent and generally by treating them administratively as part of a unit rather than as an individual on a par with any man — is the single most important factor in the inequality between the sexes.

Class analysis is incapable of incorporating such considerations, since the personal dependency of women cross-cuts the various male classes. This becomes most obvious when focusing on economic relationships within the family. Class analysis is premised on a particular set of economic relationships within society, namely a capitalist economy, and all its concepts are built upon this premise. The family is also an economic unit, but not a capitalist one. In fact, I would suggest that it is better described as a quasi-feudal institution, and it is for this reason that class concepts are inapplicable to women.

The Family as a Quasi-feudal Institution

The husband-wife relationship can be understood as a quasi-feudal relationship in so far as the wife performs personal services for her husband in exchange for protection and goods. In many countries the husband is still required by law to support his wife. In exchange, either by law or by social custom, the wife is required to perform personal services for the husband which include sexual availability, maintenance of the household, and care for the children, among others. Where there are laws which require that the wife's residence be where her husband's residence is, her mobility is restricted. She is required to move with him, if and when he moves, lest she be charged with desertion, and she may likewise not move into another residence unless she can persuade her husband to move with her. For her labour, the wife receives such goods as are necessary for her survival, namely shelter, food and clothes, and, according to circumstances, luxuries. The wife may therefore not be badly off, but she has no right to a minimum wage, even though her husband may spend a lot of money on her. In other words, she may be expensively kept, but she is not even minimally paid. This is usually the case even though the wife may actually handle the major part of family expenses. A financially dependent wife may spend money only under the constraint of a potential veto by her husband. For instance, if a wife decides that she is going to buy presents for her lover with the money that her husband gives her, the husband is quite likely to withdraw his money irrespective of the amount or the quality of labour performed by the wife. In other words, the wife does not have the power of disposing of the money in any way she sees fit. She only has as much control over purchases and expenditures as her husband is willing to grant her, and her control can be revoked for specific reasons.

A marriage is an economic relationship, but not a capitalist type of economic relationship. In Canada, a husband may not claim on his tax declaration the wages that he may have paid his wife for services rendered. Until recently, if a wife had consistently contributed labour to a 'joint' business endeavour, for example a farm or a store, which had been of such an essential nature that without her services the endeavour would not have been possible, upon divorce she had nevertheless not earned an interest in the enterprise. On the contrary, such labour contributions, although recognised as essential, were considered part of the normal duties of a wife. This is comparable to the situation of a serf who labours on his master's land, and receives some of the fruit of his labour back in the form of sustenance during work time, but who, at the completion of the relationship, has no right to any of the surplus value that has been produced. For instance, upon the death of a serf, his rented land commonly reverted to the landholder, for him to rent to a new serf, who might or might not be a direct heir of the deceased serf. This is comparable to marriage laws whereby the wife is entitled to receive the necessities of life from her husband in exchange for unpaid labour and sexual availability but in the case of conflict the law does not recognise that the wife partakes of the surplus value which has been produced within the marriage relationship through joint labour.[3] It is, therefore, inappropriate to try to analyse the economic aspects of a marital relationship in terms of an economic model which has been created for the analysis of a capitalist economic system.

We shall now consider some of the crucial concepts in class analysis and demonstrate how they are not adaptable to incorporate women, since they are not geared to combine analysis of a quasi-feudal system with analysis of a capitalist system.

1. *The Relationships of Spouses to the Means of Production*

If we wish critically to examine the relationships of spouses to the means of production we need to differentiate between spouses in one-job and in two-job couples. (It should be remembered that this criticism is geared only toward the utility of the class concept in contemporary highly industrialised societies, not in past societies.) Obviously, there are differences in analysis necessary if the wife holds a paid job or if she does not, since occupation is usually seen as the determinant factor in one's relationship to the means of production. We shall therefore consider both possibilities in turn.

(a) The Relationship of Spouses to the Means of Production in Two-job Families. We know that people tend to marry homogamously — people from the same class tend to marry each other. But do they? What this sociological theorem really means is that men tend to marry women whose fathers belong to the same social class as they themselves belong to, and it is assumed that this places women in the same class. Class membership is seen as being primarily determined by one's relationship to the means of production. This, in turn, is determined by one's occupation. If, therefore, the wife holds a paid job, whose job determines her social class? Hers, or that of her husband? Statistically speaking, women and men hold different jobs, with the women being more likely to occupy white-collar, low-pay, low-prestige service jobs, and the men being more likely to hold blue-collar 'productive' jobs and higher-paid more prestigious managerial and executive jobs (which might, however,

also be understood as service jobs). It is therefore highly probable that in two-job couples husband and wife hold jobs which are different in nature, pay, and prestige. If we identify the class membership of each spouse in terms of his/her own job, in most couples the wife would then belong to a lower class than her husband. But does this make sense in view of the fact that legally the family is treated as a unit, and that the couple during the tenure of their marriage are assumed to enjoy the fruits of their labours jointly?

In practice, the class position of the wife is often seen as being determined by the occupational position of the husband. In other words, the wife of a blue-collar worker is seen as a member of the working class, the wife of a professional is not. However, on what basis can we possibly argue that one paid job is more important than another paid job in determining one's class position? Two people sell their labour power on the labour market; in one case we declare this to be the prime indicator of that person's social class, in the other case we ignore this fundamental aspect of class position. On the other hand, if the wife is a secretary and the husband is a lawyer, the couple does not live in the lifestyle of a secretary, but in the lifestyle typical of a lawyer with a 'working wife'. To assume that the spouses belong to two classes rather than to one is as problematic as to assume that they belong to the same class.

Let us assume, for the sake of simplicity, that our couple belongs to the rare group of couples in which both spouses have equivalent jobs. It is statistically highly probable, however, that the wife is paid less than her husband (with equal amount of training and a similar job). In addition, she does most of the housework, so she works considerably longer hours than her husband for less pay. In so far as she receives less money for more labour, she is exploited more than her husband (no matter at what level they work) and belongs, if we classify her on her own basis, to a different social class from his.

(b) *The Relationship of Spouses to the Means of Production in One-job Families.* In one-job families in which the husband is the breadwinner and the wife is the housewife, the conjugal unit has always been treated as belonging to one social class. However, the relationship to the means of production is obviously fundamentally different for the wife and for the husband. He sells his labour on the labour market and in return receives money which he brings to his wife (and children). His relationship to the means of production is a direct one, hers an indirect one, in so far as she uses the money earned by him to purchase goods for the family. Their work is fundamentally different. To maintain that husband and wife belong to the same class implies a total ignorance of the actual circumstances.

The fiction that the relationship of husband and wife to the means of production is identical has been made possible by two related myths: that the relationship to property is identical for husband and wife, and that the family is a private rather than a public unit and that, therefore, whatever is being brought into the family is not changed in the process but simply consumed. Both myths will now be examined.

2. *Property within the Family*

Property is something that is owned by somebody. The myth suggests that the family — as a unit — owns property. Presumably, then, every member of the family unit shares equally in the family property. What does it mean to possess or own something? The *Encyclopedia Britannica* comments that

> Since the objects of property and the protected relationships vary among societies and over time, it is difficult to find a least common denominator of property. 'My property' probably means at a minimum that government will help me exclude others from the use or enjoyment of an object without my consent, which I may withhold except at a price. (1973, vol. 18, p.633).

Assuming that a husband and wife decide jointly on expenditures with the available money, we might assume that both husband and wife share equally in the family property. In so far as the spouses live in the same residence, eat together and do other things together, again we might assume that family property is shared. However, in practice, there are limitations to the joint ownership. The limitations apply whether or not we are dealing with a one-job or a two-job family and we shall therefore discuss both cases together, unless specifically stated otherwise. As a rule, the lifestyle is set by the breadwinner. If, therefore, the husband makes a lot of money, but wishes to live in a very modest life style, the wife is not entitled to spend above the limit set by him beyond the necessities of life.

Apart from instances of marriage breakdown where the law divides the property between the spouses according to pre-established rules, the disposition of family money is no problem for as long as the spouses agree. The real test as to who has the power to determine how family property is utilised comes in cases of disagreement. Let us assume that a couple has joint savings, and that the wife wishes to go on a world travel with the accrued savings, while the husband has no such desire. The husband will be in a position to veto the expenditure of the funds, and in this particular instance he may even be able to charge the wife with desertion if she takes her earned portion of the funds and goes away travelling for a sufficiently long period of time. Likewise if the wife wishes to use the funds in order to study, and the husband objects, often he has veto powers which prevent her from carrying out her plans. The point to be made here is that the decision-making power of the wife is, in practical terms, constrained by the inclinations, generosity, stinginess, affluence or poverty of her husband. She has the privilege of spending joint money as and when granted by him. What is granted may, however, be revoked.

Over all then, 'family property' is limited in its communal qualities in the following ways. First, the right to acquire property is vested unequally in the spouses, with the breadwinner or greater earner being able to have a greater say in the acquisition of goods. The simplest manner in which the inequality can be acted out is if the husband controls the bank account in which earnings are deposited: there need never be any overt disagreement; if he disapproves of the proposed use of the money he can simply fail to hand the money over for that specific purpose. Second, the right to dispose of property is vested unequally in the spouses. If assets are registered in the husband's name, as is a plausible assumption, he can sell them unilaterally, but she cannot. For example, if the car is in his name, he can sell it, she cannot, although she may feel that the money is needed more for some other item. Third, in the case of break-up of marriages, the property tends to be awarded to the person who has made the greater *direct* financial contribution towards its acquisition. Some legal systems recognise the indirect contributions of the financially weaker partner, usually the wife, by splitting the assets acquired during the duration of the marriage between the two, but most legal systems do not recompense wives, especially housewives, in a manner proportionate to their labours.

To call assets 'family property' with the implication that they are shared equally by the spouses (nobody pretends that they belong equally to the children of a marriage) is, therefore, a euphemism. Consequently, it is not justified to assume that women and men within the family unit have the same relationship to property, whether or not the wife has a paying job. On this basis also, then, women cannot be counted to belong to the same class as their husbands, and even less to the same class as their fathers. Single women, on the other hand, can be treated as members of a social class on the same basis as married or unmarried men.

3. *The Private-Public Distinction*

One of the reasons why family structure has been seen as insignificant for evaluating people's social position and why housework has until recently been totally ignored when discussing the social division of labour is that the division of labour within the family is not seen as a social division of labour (since the family is presumed to share equally goods brought into it as a unit, rather than unequally among various individuals who make up the family). Things that happen in the family are seen as things that happen in a private domain which is irrelevant for an understanding of social mechanisms. This approach denies that the division of labour within the family is a significant aspect of the division of labour within the entire society, and assumes that things are consumed within the family without being appreciably altered. It is only when we take the individual rather than the family as the unit of analysis that we can start critically to examine the appropriateness of various stratification theories for women's place in society. The claim that the division of labour within the family is non-social, since it occurs within a private sector without any value being added to the product that is being processed within the family, must be seen as an arbitrary rather than a factually based argument.

The treatment of the family as a private unit finds its expression in class analysis in two specific ways: first, the view that housework is non-productive labour and, second, the related view that housework produces only use-values, not exchange-values. Both of these statements assume that the contemporary family is only a consuming unit and not a producing unit. We shall briefly examine both statements.

4. *Housework as the Production of Use-values rather than Exchange-values*

Three concepts are important to understand the view that housework is the production of use-values rather than exchange-values, namely value, use-value and exchange-value. The value of a product is directly proportionate to its socially necessary time of production. The use-value of a product is inherent in the product itself (e.g. clothes keep us warm, they make us look good, etc.). The exchange-value of a product in a money economy is expressed in the amount of money people are willing to pay for the commodity.

Any product may have an exchange-value and a use-value but it need not have both. It may have a use-value without an exchange-value, although it cannot have an exchange-value without a use-value. A thing may further have use-value without having value (i.e. it is not socially produced), for example in the case of air, primary forest, etc. Finally, a thing may be a product of human labour without being a commodity. Whoever produces something to satisfy his or her own needs has produced use-value but not a commodity. In order to produce a commodity one needs to produce not just use-value, but use-value for somebody else, social use-value. So far Marx (Marx, 1953, pp.39-45). To this Engels adds by way of a parenthetical explanation that it does not suffice to produce use-value for just anybody – e.g., the medieval peasant who produces corn for his liege-lord does not produce a commodity. In order to become a commodity a product must be transferred through an exchange to somebody else for whom the commodity has some use-value (Marx, 1953, p.45).

Now let us consider the case of housework. If a man hires a housekeeper, he pays her for her services. Her labour, therefore, has not only use-value but also exchange-value. If and when he marries her, he is not legally entitled to pay her for her labour (he cannot claim the pay on his tax deduction), although he is obliged to maintain her. Assuming that the work she does as a wife is identical to the work she did as a housekeeper, the character of her work has not changed, only her civil status has changed. The work she does is still socially necessary work, but as a housewife she is no longer paid for it. The real exchange-value (as determined by the price the user of her labours would have to pay were she not his wife) is taken from her. The distinction between use-value and exchange-value hides the fact that a theft has occurred. If housework is performed by a person for somebody other than her husband and she receives pay for it, it is deemed to have exchange-value. If the identical work is performed by a married woman for her husband, it is presumed to have no exchange-value. The flaw is that for that portion of the housework that the husband feels he cannot do himself and for which he would, consequently, be willing to pay were his wife to refuse to perform the work, the work itself in an abstract sense does have an exchange-value, but the performer of the work does not receive its equivalency value. In other words, because the family is a quasi-feudal institution (and Engels' example of the medieval peasant makes the point quite strongly) we cannot analyse the value of housework in terms of exchange-value and use-value, since these concepts are grounded in a different type of economic system.

5. *Housework as Non-productive Labour*

According to Seecombe, housework is necessary but unproductive labour. He sees labour as productive if it is conducted in direct relation to capital and if it produces surplus value (Seecombe, 1974). Therefore, housework is seen as unproductive, since it is not wage labour (that is, it has no direct relation to capital) and since it does not produce any surplus value.

However, let us again consider the work of a housekeeper. Her work is paid and is thereby not different from the labour of other workers (e.g. secretaries or telephone operators) in its relation to capital. Further, surplus value can be defined as the increment in value that is generated through the labours that have transformed certain materials (e.g. flour, eggs, milk, and spices) into a new product (e.g. a cake). The surplus value refers to that portion of·money that the capitalist retains after an exchange has occurred and after necessary materials, labour, and capital costs have been accounted for. That is, surplus value is a concept that makes sense only within the context of commodity production. In so far as the housewife is not paid, the product of her work has value, but no surplus value. On the other hand, if this same product is produced by a baker and sold in a bakery shop, it constitues a commodity which presumably generates surplus value.

It is not, therefore, anything inherent in the product or in the work process that makes housework non-productive in the Marxist sense, but it is because of her marital status that the work of the housewife is considered non-productive. It is therefore incorrect to say that housework is unproductive; rather the work performed by a housewife, i.e. by a married woman who works without pay, is classified as unproductive in so far as her labour does not entitle her to a minimum pay. This does not negate the fact that some products are produced and some services rendered within the household. In this sense, one could understand the modern family not only as a unit of consumption but also as a unit of production in the way in which other service establishments such as barber shops, typing pools, catering services, etc. produce goods and offer services. However, the point is not to argue that housework is productive, but rather that the definition of productivity is based on circular reasoning. By definition, only what is paid for can be productive; therefore, if something is not being paid for, it must be unproductive. This is where the problem lies.

Class Analysis and Patriarchy

When Marxist scholars discuss class society, there are several simultaneous thrusts to the discussion. One is simply an attempt to analyse stratification in industrialised societies. Second is an implicit evaluation of class society as bad. Third is an implicit change orientation: class society should be abolished and replaced with a classless society. And fourth, class structure is seen as the root problem of human relations, hence the self-definition as 'radical' (going to the roots of human relational problems). From the latter perception it follows that before we can meaningfully attempt to solve any other social problem, we need to redress the imbalance inherent in class society. Patriarchy is, therefore, defined by most Marxists as a second-order problem that can only be successfully tackled after we have solved the problem posed by class divisions.

One exception to this view is presented by Hartmann (1976) who has placed patriarchy beside capitalism in an attempt to explain the persistence of patriarchal structures in capitalist and pre-capitalist societies. Although I do not agree with the argument as elaborated,[4] I do agree with the emphasis on patriarchy and capitalism as two co-existent but independent variables. For patriarchy does, of course, exist in non-capitalist countries, at least those which are non-capitalist by self-definition, namely contemporary socialist countries.

For non-Marxist scholars, some measure of social class, namely some operationalisation of SES, is the most fundamental variable for explaining human behaviours. Whether we consider Marxist or non-Marxist class analysis, the feeling in both cases is that class membership is the most important explanatory variable with which we can presently deal.

We have now seen that class analysis, no matter which viewpoint is taken, is not able adequately to incorporate women. Either we must conceptualise women as a distinct social class, which destroys class analysis since women, who on the basis of their relationship to their husband would belong to one social class, would as workers themselves belong to a second social class and as women to a third social class. Alternatively, we have seen that it is equally problematic to subsume the wife under her husband's class membership. In the case of women, it is not only the paid work they do which determines their status; their family status is also important. The family and the economy are both important factors.

The family is an economic unit, but involves economic relationships of a different nature from those around which class analysis is geared. In its internal logic, class analysis is incapable of incorporating an analysis of the position of women in the family, since the central concepts developed and used for analysis — exchange-value and use-value, production and consumption, the relationship to the means of production, occupation and wages — are premised on a capitalist rather than a quasi-feudal type of relationship.

In other words, class analysis cannot incorporate sex stratification, because its internal logic makes it a closed system. Sex stratification, however, is real and universally present, whereas class stratification is not universally present. Not all societies (e.g. some primitive societies) have social classes but they all have a stratification by sex. In this sense we can see sex as a more fundamental stratifying variable than social class. Clearly, we must start to reconceptualise our entire stratification model. That, I am sure, will take many decades to come.

Notes

1. This fallacy of arguing for an upwards evaluation without changes in the social structure becomes obvious when we reverse the sex of such statements. Erikson's statement, for example, would read as follows:

> Since a man is never not-a-man, he can see his long-range goals only in those modes of activity which include and integrate his natural dispositions. An emancipated man thus does not necessarily accept comparisons with more 'passive' female proclivities as a measure of his equivalence, even if and after it has become quite clear that he can match woman's performance and competence in most spheres of achievement. True equality can only mean the right to be uniquely creative.

Talking about emancipation, equivalence, matching of performance and competence of men in a setting of male superiority is ridiculous. Yet how can we change the evaluation of women's activities unless we change also the evaluation of men's activities?

2. Perhaps the case becomes more convincing when we consider the case of domestic servants in nineteenth-century Europe and America, and in present-day developing countries. Domestic servants may live in the same house with their employers and female servants may be sexually exploited by their male employers, yet hardly anybody would want to argue that this indicates social proximity between domestic servants and their employers.

3. In Canada, family law is under provincial rather than under federal jurisdiction. In 1978, the Province of Ontario introduced a new family law according to which the matrimonial home and some other necessities of life are shared between ex-spouses in case of divorce. This introduces a new variation into family economic relationships which is more removed from a quasi-feudal model, but which is no closer to a capitalist economic model.

4. According to Hartmann (1976), before the advent of capitalism a patriarchal system was established in which men controlled the labour of women and children in the family. In so doing they learned the techniques of hierarchical control and organisation, which were translated into an impersonal, indirect system of social control of women once changes in the economy and in the form

of government resulted in a widespread private-public distinction. Job segregation by sex is the primary mechanism in capitalist society that maintains the superiority of men over women. '... the hierarchical domestic division of labour is perpetuated by the labour market, and vice versa. This process is the present outcome of the continuing interaction of two interlocking systems, capitalism and patriarchy' (p.139). While one must certainly agree that patriarchy and capitalism are two independent, interlocking variables, Hartmann leaves unclear how men transmit the techniques of control and domination to boys when both boys and girls are raised by women due to the domestic division of labour.

References

Ambert, Anne-Marie. *Sex Structure* (2nd. rev. enl. edn, Don Mills, Longman Canada, 1976).

Bell, Norman W. *Domestic Murders in Canada*, 1961-1974 (monograph published by the Judicial Statistics Division, Statistics Canada, Ottawa, 1977).

Benston, Margaret. 'The Political Economy of Women's Liberation', *Monthly Review*, vol. 21, no. 4 (1969), pp.13-27.

Berreman, Gerald D. 'The Concept of Caste', *International Encyclopedia of the Social Sciences*, vol. 11 (USA, Crowell and Macmillan, 1968), pp. 333-9.

Bose, Christine, 'Social Status of the Homemaker' (paper presented at the American Sociological Association, New York, 1976).

Chan, Kwok B. 'Wife-Beating: Some Substantive and Theoretical Issues'. (unpublished paper, 1977).

Collins, Randall. 'A Conflict Theory of Sexual Stratification', in Hans Peter Dreitzel (ed.), *Family, Marriage, and the Struggle of the Sexes* (New York, Macmillan Co., 1972), pp.53-79.

Eichler, Margrit, with the assistance of Neil Guppy and Janet Siltanen. 'The Prestige of the Occupation Housewife', in Patrician Marchak (ed.), *The Working Sexes. Symposium Papers on the Effects of Sex on Women at Work* (Vancouver, Institute of Industrial Relations, 1977), pp. 151-75.

Erikson, Erik H. 'Inner and Outer Space: Reflections on Womanhood', in Robert Jay Lifton (ed.), *The Woman in America* (Boston, Beacon Press, 1964), pp.1-26.

Glazer-Malbin, Nona. 'Capitalism and the Class Crisis for Women' (paper presented at the Pacific Sociological Association, San Diego, 1976).

Hacker, Helen Mayer. 'Women as a Minority Group', *Social Forces* 30 (Oct. 1951), pp.60-9.

Hartmann, Heidi. 'Capitalism, Patriarchy, and Job Segregation by Sex', *Signs*, vol. 1, no. 3, part 2, pp.137-69.

Martin, Del. *Battered Wives* (San Francisco, Glide Publications, 1976).

Marx, Karl. *Das Kapital. Kritik der politischen Ökonomie* (Berlin, Dietz Verlag, 1953).

Myrdal, Gunnar, *An American Dilemma. The Negro Problem and Modern Democracy* (New York and London, Harper and Bros, 1944).

Ossowski, Stanislaw. *Class Structure in the Social Consciousness* (London, Routledge & Kegan Paul, 1963).

Pizzey, Erin, *Scream Quietly or the Neighbors Will Hear* (London, If Books, 1974).

Pleck, Elizabeth. 'Wife-Beating in Nineteenth Century America' (unpublished paper, 1977).

"Property", *Encyclopedia Britannica*, vol. 18 (1973), p.633.

Seecombe, Wally. 'The Housewife and Her Labour under Capitalism', *New Left Review,* no. 83 (1974).

Steinmetz, Suzanne K. 'Violence Between Family Members', *Marriage and Family Review* vol. 1, no. 3 (May/June 1978), pp.1-16.

Steinmetz, Suzanne K. and Murray A. Straus (eds.). *Violence in the Family* (New York, Dodd, Mead & Co., 1974).

Whitehurst, Robert N. 'Violence in Separation and Divorce: Process and Structure' (unpublished paper, 1977).

Zuker, Marvin A. and June Callwood. *The Law is Not for Women* (Toronto, Pitman Publishing, 1976).

5 CONCLUSION: WHITHER FEMINISM?

For an academic, feminism has at least two components: a practical-political one and a scientific one. Scientific feminism is critical of the social sciences as they are presently constituted and supplies the framework for an alternative perspective. Feminism in a practical-political sense is critical of the prevailing sex structure, and supplies a framework for changing it. In this chapter we shall discuss aspects of a feminist scientific perspective, and some desirable changes that are geared towards the elimination of the sexual double standard.

Scientific Feminism

For non-feminists, the adjective 'feminist' has the connotation of 'unscientific', indicating the presence of an ideology, of a previously established value commitment of a researcher or teacher which works to the detriment of other more traditional value commitments and is hence seen as being liable to distort reality by a biased emphasis. Likewise, for a feminist, non-feminist science has exactly these connotations.

Therefore it is obviously necessary to understand what feminist science means. 'Feminist science' is a term that makes sense only in the context of an overwhelmingly sexist science. If science were not sexist there would be no need for a feminist science, in fact feminist science would not be 'thinkable'. Feminist science is non-sexist. In other words, we need to define sexist science in order to grasp the intent and nature of feminist science. Sexist science is characterised by the following aspects:

1. Women are to a large degree ignored, yet conclusions and theories are phrased in such general terms that they purport to be applicable to all of humanity.
2. If women are considered, they tend to be considered only in so far as they are important for and related to men, not by virtue of their own importance as human subjects.
3. Where both sexes are considered, the male is generally taken as the norm, the female as the deviation from the norm.
4. Sexist content is mirrored in sexist language, as reflected, for instance, in the use of the generic he and the generic man.

5. Sexist science is full of preconceived notions concerning a masculine and feminine nature. Consequently, identical behaviours or situations involving women and men are described and analysed differently according to sex. In other words, we find a consistent double standard within sexist science.
6. By using sexist notions of human nature, and employing a double standard in interpreting findings, sexist science itself becomes one contributing factor in the maintenance of the sex structure from which it arose in the first place and in which it is grounded.

Over all, then, sexist science seriously distorts reality and contributes to the continued existence of factors facilitating distortion not only where women are concerned, but also where men are concerned, since ignoring or misrepresenting half of humanity must by necessity lead to inappropriate generalisations about the human condition in general.

Feminist science, then, is presently concerned with two tasks: first, to point out the various ways in which currently accepted scientific methods and theories are, in fact, sexist and thereby distorting, and second, to try to devise new methods and theories which will not have the weaknesses that non-feminist science has. The second task is, clearly, only possible after the first has been achieved and this is where most of the activity still needs to be taking place. Only after we have cleared away the sexist rubble that is lying all over the place will we be able to construct new, non-sexist ways of describing and analysing social reality.

Feminist science, therefore, is at its very beginning – we are still in the process of clearing the field in order to be able to imagine what sort of buildings we might eventually wish to erect in the place of the ones we are trying to pull down. Consequently, most precepts of feminist science still take the form of 'don't's rather than 'do's.

The 'Don't's and 'Do's of Feminist Science

The aim of feminist science is to create a science that accounts for the behaviour of all humans, female as well as male. Therefore, any empirical statement on the basis of which a theoretical statement is made must include female as well as male subjects. Likewise, any theory that purports to be general must be capable of explaining female as well as male behaviour. We must not take male behaviour as the norm against which female behaviour is evaluated, but must identify our norms such that they are truly human norms.

In order to recognise whether or not theoretical or empirical statements are applicable to both women and men we must, as a necessary precondition, de-masculinise our language. In other words, we must not continue to use male pronouns and nouns as generic terms (e.g. the history of mankind instead of the history of humanity, or man is a political animal instead of people are political animals) because this usage, while it is an expression of sexism at the level of language, hides the sexism at the level of theory. Only when we specify consistently that we wish to talk about people rather than men will we realise how little applicable most of what is being said is, in fact, to people, and to what vast degree it is, indeed, only applicable to men in a literal sense.

Demasculinising our language is no more than a necessary precondition; it does not overcome the problem of the exclusion of women. It merely helps us to recognise when women are in fact being excluded, which is by no means as easy a task as it may seen, as it is extremely hard to break through established thought patterns. The best example in this context is, perhaps, the effort to realise that our prehistories have so far been primarily concerned with reconstructing the origin of *man*. For an attempt to reconstruct the origin of humanity, see Boulding (1976).

Further, we must cease to identify cultures, values, norms, character traits and behaviour as masculine and feminine. 'Feminine' and 'masculine' should be used only as labels for empirically established configurations of variables which are differentiated by sex, never as generally valid descriptors. The reason is that masculinity and femininity are not generated by innate factors, but are the results of social factors. Therefore, with changing social conditions, the meaning of masculinity and femininity constantly changes, as does the meaning, for instance, of what is deviant and what is normal. Just as we cannot have a notion of normality which is not culturally specific, so we cannot have a universal notion of femininity or masculinity. If we deny the cultural specificity of notions of masculinity and femininity, we have entered the realm of ideological rather than scientific statements. In particular, we must cease to devise and use masculinity-femininity scales, since they primarily symbolise the ossification of sex role stereotypes. We must also cease to think of women as objects that link men to men or as people attached to men, and must start to understand women as subjects in history, and as actors in the same sense in which men are actors.

We must cease to use a methodology that discards items and results because they do not 'differentiate' between the sexes. For instance, in survey research concerned with sex differences only such items for which the answers of women and men differ tend to be retained. This introduces a systematically distorting factor with cumulative effects. As Maccoby and Jacklin (1974, pp.4-6) have pointed out, the tendency on the part of researchers to stress sex differences rather than similarities is compounded by the tendency of editors and publishers to publish findings only if they show sex differences rather than similarities. In fact, a finding of 'no sex difference' may be regarded as not a finding at all, and the already existing distortion in the data which stresses the differences rather than the similarities between the sexes is thereby further amplified.

We must also cease to compartmentalise qualities of actions as if they were mutually exclusive. Most predominantly, we must cease to treat rationality and emotionality (or instrumentality and expressiveness) as two mutually exclusive qualities of actions and must instead treat them as separate continua that vary independently and can be applied to any single action. If we scrub the floor, we are presumably engaging in a purposeful activity of cleaning and, depending on circumstances, our emotions may be engaged lightly or strongly in a negative or positive direction. The same is true for kissing, which may be used as a manipulative activity for wheedling out something that is desired from somebody else, in which case the action involved would be geared towards some instrumental goal and not towards mutual emotional gratification. Its emotional quality in such a case would be slight, at least for one of the actors involved.

Further, we must cease to treat the family primarily as a functional unit, and start to think of it as a complex pattern of relationships between different role incumbents: wife, husband, child, parent, exspouse, step-parent, sibling, etc. We must stop assuming that what is detrimental or beneficial to one member of the family unit is necessarily the same to another member. We must recognise that the family in general may be the most supportive or the most destructive kind of social group — and sometimes the same family may even be both.

We must start to define work as all work, whether paid or unpaid, and whether performed by women or by men. Presence or absence of pay is just one way in which work can be categorised; for most analyses, especially when we are discussing the functions of work, it is not a particularly useful way of categorising work. Perhaps a more meaningful way of categorising work would be in terms of its social necessity or lack of necessity, or perhaps by its degree of social utility. Socially necessary work would include some work that is presently unpaid work, and would exclude some work that is presently paid work. An example

of socially unnecessary paid work would be some aspects of bureau-
cratic work, or jobs which could be better handled by machines but
which are retained because of negotiated contracts, while socially
necessary but at present mostly unpaid work would certainly include
childcare and the care of sick or physically dependent people such as
elderly and/or handicapped people.

Finally, we must cease to understand sex role socialisation as a
normal, healthy, necessary building block of one's personality. Instead,
we should start to perceive it as a systematic form of crippling people,
analogous to some socially approved forms of physical crippling, for
instance in the Chinese practice of binding feet. Sex roles, as presently conceived, have very little to do with sexuality, yet this is the
only acceptable basis on which people should have strong notions concerning the nature and significance of their sex. So long as their sex has
all sorts of physically irrelevant social connotations, I do not think that
we can expect people to have a self-image which incorporates their sex
in a positive sense.

What is perhaps most important is that we must cease to classify
people in terms of social classes as defined at present, not because social
inequality does not exist for it demonstrably does, but because class
analysis is by its internal logic incapable of incorporating women and is
therefore unacceptable as a tool of analysis.

So where do all these 'don't's leave us? With a strange dilemma,
certainly, the strangest of which concerns the use of the variable 'sex'.
Explaining matters by sex may be both the most useful and the most
dangerous manner of explanation imaginable. The answer to the
dilemma lies, I think, in seeing sex as a variable that must be used in a
dialectical manner; if this is not done its introduction may be as detrimental as the neglect of it, as shown by masculinity-femininity scales,
literature on sex role socialisation, writings on adrogyny, discussions
of cross-cultural sex differences, etc. The problem with most of the
work in these areas is precisely that it overextends the explanatory
capacity of the variable sex.

We must perceive all analyses concerning sex as a two-stage process. As a first step, it is necessary to chart the presence of sex differences and similarities in all kinds of situations. Thus, in a descriptive
manner, sex can and must be used as an explanatory variable. For
instance, sex 'explains' a lot of the difference in terms of salary levels
between employees in similar occupations. The explanation provided
by this type of statement is of a probabilistic kind only. However, we
must never use sex as a variable in a causal sense in order to explain

social facts. That is, we must not accept an equation of a description of sex differences with their explanation. For instance, we may empirically observe that women who are offered executive chances for promotion are more reluctant to accept them than men. If so, the likelihood of accepting offered promotions would be an observed sex difference. Sex has been used as an explanatory variable in a probabilistic sense. However, this observation tells us nothing about the reasons why women are less likely to accept offered promotions. A possible explanation might be that as women move into higher positions, they encounter fewer and fewer other women and increased male solidarity and hostility against themselves, which makes such positions very lonely to hold. The explanation for not accepting a certain type of social position would, in such a case, be lack of social support for the potential incumbent of the position, a reason which would, under different circumstances, be equally applicable to men. In social policy terms, a move to counteract this effect might involve promotion of a whole group of women together to a higher level. An observed sex difference has, therefore, been explained by a non-sexual, non-biological, social factor. If we fail to take that second step and do not deal with sex in a dialectical manner, we fail to explain anything at all and, worse than that, we may create new sexual stereotypes ourselves.

A feminist programme of research must, therefore, include both the charting and description of sex differences and similarities, and an attempt to explain the observed sex differences in a non-sexual manner.

Practical-Political Issues in Feminism

The over-all goal of the feminist movement can be summarised in one simple sentence: to abolish the sexual double standard. This seemingly modest request incorporates within itself a social revolution that would leave no aspect of our social lives untouched, which is simply another way of saying that the sexual double standard is deeply ingrained in all parts of our present social life. It is part of our legal structure, part of our economic structure, part of our educational system; it underlies our political system, is constantly evident in the mass media, and the contemporary family is firmly built on a multi-layer double standard. The double standard is also manifested in attitudes and social practices at a formal and informal level. We can empirically demonstrate the existence of the double standard in all these forms. Talking about its elimination, however, is not a simple matter, even leaving aside practical difficulties. Let us take a simple, concrete example and examine it from the perspective of the double standard.

Let us assume a company has a policy of hiring only males for positions of executive power (unfortunately by no means an unrealistic assumption). This policy is being challenged, and the firm consequently drops it as a policy. In a formalistic-legal sense, this would indicate the abolition of the sexual double standard. Suitably qualified women can now be appointed to executive positions along with equally qualified men. However, since the abolition of the formal policy does not result in any immediate appointments of women in such positions, little has really changed. Let us now assume the firm *wants* to hire women in such positions, and actively searches for women who meet those requirements which are defined as necessary for the vacant positions. It does not find any. We have now to turn to an examination of those requirements which are defined as necessary for the job. Are they really necessary? Or are they themselves simply the result of a thinking which does not see women in positions of authority?

For instance, height requirements for police officers are an example in point, since they tend to favour men who on the average tend to be taller than women, and since there is no necessary connection between being a good police officer and meeting a certain height level. A precondition for employment may, therefore, be in itself a manifestation of a double standard.

Let us assume that the firm in our example abolishes all sexually biased requirements that it may have had, in its attempt to attract women into positions of authority.

Now let us make some other assumptions. Let us assume that all potential female candidates for the open positions are women with dependent children (this is not a very realistic assumption, of course, since the potential female candidates are likely to be unmarried and childless or married and childless) and that one of the characteristics of the executive positions is that the executives must be able to work long hours. This, let us assume, is due to the nature of the business conducted, a necessity of the job, and is not negotiable. The firm has now gone as far as it can as one single firm in its attempts to abolish its own internal double standard, and yet women are still affected by other aspects of the double standard, since it turns out that they have (and this is, unfortunately, a realistic assumption) the primary responsibility for childcare. Because the family structure is based on a double standard, and children are seen not only as more the mother's responsibility than the father's but also as a private rather than a public responsibility, the potential female candidates are still labouring under a handicap which their male rivals do not have.

To identify a double standard, therefore, we must ask ourselves a sequence of questions concerning any observed social difference between the sexes. What is the immediate cause of the differential? What are the various mediate causes?

To change only one aspect of the social structure, for instance by abolishing the legal double standard (e.g. by creating equal access to family property according to each spouse's financial and labour contribution, by eliminating restrictions on female workers and extending protective labour legislation to men, by ensuring equal pay for work of equal value, by assigning child custody on the basis of the interest of the child and not the sex of the parent, etc.), we have taken a necessary, but by no means sufficient step towards the abolition of the sexual double standard. For instance, the right to vote and to be elected has been held by women in most countries for about half a century now, but actually to get elected into a political office is incomparably more difficult for a woman than for a man.

By creating change in one sector of society we are necessarily creating social strain, since other, interrelated sectors will not change at the same time or even in the same directions. Given certain types of situations, laws which are based on a sexual double standard may, in the short run, be more advantageous for women than laws which treat the sexes equally. For instance, divorce laws which require a man to support his ex-wife for an indefinite period of time after divorce are clearly based on a double standard. However, any attempts to change such laws must recognise that the chances of a woman who has been a housewife for, let us say, twenty or thirty years finding a job are extremely slim. By contrast, the man does not need to search for a new job after divorce. It would be unrealistic to expect that a woman who has been economically dependent for an extended period of time can suddenly start supporting herself when the infrastructure for such self-support is missing. On the other hand, if the ex-wife is quite young she should clearly be expected to support herself after divorce.

Abolishing the double standard is, therefore, neither a simple nor a quick matter. It is a programme for a social revolution which is comparable in import to the Industrial Revolution with all the consequent changes in social life.

Some of the currently identified issues in feminism can be grouped under the headings of:

1. the elimination of sexism from teaching materials;
2. control over one's own body;
3. sexual justice;

4. Economic justice.

1. *The Elimination of Sexism from Teaching Materials*

A great deal of effort has been expended in identifying the presence of sexism in teaching materials at the elementary, secondary and post-secondary level. In a sense this book belongs partially to the category of efforts that try to identify sexist assumptions in teaching materials — in this case at the post-secondary level. Attempts in this direction include the elaboration of non-sexist materials which picture girls and boys, women and men in a variety of roles and contexts. This is probably the least contentious, least threatening and most successful undertaking of feminism so far, at least in North America.

2. *Control over One's Own Body*

Control over one's own body is an elementary aspect of human autonomy and dignity. While we are all, women and men alike, affected by the way the medical establishment treats us, women have some special difficulties to overcome in gaining control over their bodies due to the way the (overwhelmingly male) medical establishment regards their sexuality. Consequently, demands of feminists have centred on making free, early and complete sex education available to both girls and boys (women and men where necessary), and on the provision of access to contraception where desired and necessary. Where contraception has failed, because of ignorance or incomplete protection, abortion is required as a last resort to prevent enforced parenthood.

Women in North America are mainly treated by male doctors. The Ontario Human Rights Code in general prohibits discrimination on the basis of sex when hiring, but does allow it in the case of some *bona fide* occupations. Nevertheless, most gynaecologists and obstetricians are men, although I cannot think of a single other occupation in which the sex of the practitioner could be of more importance. The fact that obstetrics and gynaecology are in male hands has had some very definite effects on the way medicine has defined the birth process and other aspects of women's sexuality. Over all, the process of giving birth has been masculinised, with the effect that control has been taken away from the woman involved. Rather than be treated as the major actor, she has been defined and is treated as a passive patient of the male doctor.

A very important series of feminist demands, therefore, focuses on the return of control to women in the process of giving birth, and on the giving of information to women concerning their sexuality, so that informed consent can be given if and when remedial intervention should become necessary.

3. *Sexual Justice*

Demands for sexual justice take at least three forms: (a) demands to decriminalise prostitution, (b) demands to change the legal and practical circumstances surrounding cases of rape, and (c) demands for an end to discrimination against homosexuals, especially lesbians.

(a) Decriminalisation of Prostitution. Prostitution and rape are at the very core of the sexual double standard (cf. Eichler, 1977). Both would be unthinkable in a society free of it. The sexual double standard involves differential standards for sexual conduct on the part of women and men. In almost all societies in which it exists men are accorded greater sexual freedom than women. Presuming the sexual activity is predominantly heterosexual, this greater sexual freedom for men needs the presence of some special group of women who will satisfy the greater sexual demands of men. This group is, of course, what we call prostitutes, women who engage in sexual activity for money. To take part in prostitution as client or prostitute presupposes that the persons involved see sex as a service rendered by a woman to a man, rather than as the exchange of mutual gratifications and an expression of emotional closeness and tenderness. Sex for money is a business, and usually it is regarded as a shameful business. Prostitutes constitute the direct product of a double standard which allows different degrees of sexual freedom to women and men, and they are also the foremost victims. Having been defined as that group of women who render sexual services for pay, they are then blamed for doing what the sexual system has pushed them into doing. In the process, sex is bifurcated into a 'good' and a 'bad' variety.

The 'good' variety takes place within marriage or by two unmarried mutually consenting adults who engage in sexual activity for love rather than for pecuniary reasons. The 'bad' variety enables men to have a higher degree of sexual activity than most women, keeps 'good' women practising 'good' sex only, and takes place in exchange for money. 'Bad' sex is seen as socially reprehensible, but only for the women who render the services, not for the men who create the prostitutes by paying for their services, nor for society which through a sexual double standard created the preconditions in which prostitution can develop. The legal system periodically punishes prostitutes with fines, imprisonment, harassment, and lack of protection when it is needed, but does not likewise punish the clients. This is somewhat reminiscent of seal hunting — the moral blame attaches solely to the hunters rather than to the wearers of fur coats who through their demand for fur products create the preconditions for seal hunting and other forms of fur collection by making it a profitable business.

In a society without a double standard, sex for money, if it existed, would either not be punished at all, or else both procurer and client would receive the same punishment, whatever that might be.

(b) Rape. Rape in Canada is defined as follows:

> A male person commits rape when he has sexual intercourse with a female person who is not his wife,
> (a) without her consent, or
> (b) with her consent if the consent
> (i) is extorted by threats or fear of bodily harm,
> (ii) is obtained by personating her husband, or
> (iii) is obtained by false and fraudulent representations as to the nature and quality of the act. (Criminal Code, Rev. Statutes, 1970, Chapter C-34, 143)

Further,

> Every male person who has sexual intercourse with a female person who
> (a) is not his wifé
> (b) is of previously chaste character, and
> (c) is fourteen years of age or more and is under the age of sixteen years,
> whether or not he believes that she is sixteen years of age or more is guilty of an indictable offence and is liable to imprisonment for five years. (Criminal Code, Rev. Statutes, 1970, Chapter C-34m, 146 (2))

If a male has intercourse with a woman under the age of fourteen, he is guilty of rape no matter what the circumstances.

What is noteworthy in these statutes are the following aspects of the law:

1. a man cannot rape his wife,
2. a man cannot rape a man,

3. a woman cannot rape either a woman or a man,
4. the man is guilty in the case of intercourse with a woman under 14 even if she lied about her age,
5. the man is guilty in the case of intercourse with a woman between the age of 14 and 16 even if she lied about her age, provided she is of previously chaste character — in other words, if she has had intercourse before, his act is defined as socially acceptable; otherwise, it is socially unacceptable.

To translate these provisions into statements about the sexes, the underlying assumptions of these statutes is that the sexual act is something that is done by the man to the woman, not an act that is freely engaged in by both sexes. An older woman is not guilty of rape if she seduces a boy under the age of 14 or a boy of previously chaste character between the ages of 14 and 16! The notion of the male acting upon the female is firmly anchored in the language which describes the sex act; for instance, intercourse is described as the penetration of the vagina by the penis. Another way of describing the act might be the swallowing of the penis by the vagina — in which case the female would be depicted as the active partner, and not the passive partner.

Another underlying assumption is, further, that sexual intercourse is inherently more dangerous for a woman of tender age than for a man of tender age (rather than, for instance, assault, or the possibility of pregnancy).

Finally, in practice only a woman 'of chaste character' can be raped, as explicitly stated in the statute specifying the occurrence of rape for 14-16 year olds, and as implicitly shown in rape conviction cases. Although the Canadian law has been altered such that evidence on the victim's sexual conduct is no longer automatically admissible as evidence, when there is a suggestion that the rape victim had engaged in previous intercourse with the rapist, or with a fair number of other men, it is extremely unlikely that the rapist, even though nobody would question the occurrence of the crime, would be convicted of it, the assumption apparently being that a woman who engages in sex frequently has no right to refuse it when she wishes to. It is highly unlikely that a rapist who has raped a prostitute would be convicted — in fact, prostitutes are as 'unrapeable' for all men as wives are for their husbands.

The legal interpretation of sexual intercourse, as represented in the extreme case of rape, is, therefore, far from seeing sexual intercourse as an act that occurs between equals. Feminists have long argued that the sexual component of rape should be de-emphasised and the assault aspect emphasised. Rape is a particularly brutal form of assaulting somebody, and whether or not previous intercourse has occurred with the same or other men is entirely irrelevant to this fact. A woman who is sexually active has as great a right to autonomous control over her own body as a woman who is not sexually active or one who is active only with her husband. It is therefore necessary to conceive of rape as one form of assault, to consider the previous sexual conduct of the victim as entirely irrelevant, and to treat the rapist as any other violent assaulter is treated.

(c) Lesbianism and Feminism. Sexual attitudes are at present in the process of being re-formed. While there is probably no drastic change in sexual behaviour (there has always been pre-marital, post-marital, and extra-marital sex) there is a definite attempt on the part of organised groups to change the evaluation of various forms of sexual behaviour. Among these organised groups are those who wish to end discrimination against homosexuals (gay liberation) and promote the idea of homosexuality as one form of sexual behaviour that should be as socially acceptable as other forms of sexual behaviour. Feminism, in particular, has some strong and vocal groups who argue for the right of women to choose to be lesbians, some going even further to argue that one cannot be a feminist if one is heterosexually active. The analogy sometimes used is that one cannot fight the French (British, Americans, Japanese, what have you) during the day and sleep with them during the night. The discussion has, at times, become so tangled that it may be useful to try to disentangle part of it.

Lesbianism seems to be feared by both men and straight women alike. Radical feminist lesbians question the necessity for female-male association in every form and manifestation, not only the more conventional types of family relations. They are thus supplying a needed corrective for dependent female-male behaviour patterns. On the other hand, these lesbians have elevated their sexual preference to a political struggle that denies the possibility of male-female love relations not only for themselves but for every other woman as well. If and when that occurs, a confusion between economic and political dependence as they interfere with love relations (which must be based on essential equivalence) and the possibility of love in an abstract sense has taken place. If economic and political equality were achieved (and at present this is not the case for the majority of people, although a few individual women can live in a relationship of economic and political symmetry or even superiority within their own primary grouping, whether this be a family or some other form of grouping) love should again be possible between the sexes, and perhaps be possible for many people for the first time. Female and male homosexuality would, in that case, be only one way in which people may express their sexuality — heterosexual contacts need not be feared by either sex when both are equal.

To focus all attention on the physical aspects of sexuality is to forget that physical sex relations are problematic at the collective level only because other sex relations — economic, political, social, philosophical, psychological, etc. — are problematic. As a form of political protest, lesbianism is not likely to be successful, since it does not represent a strategy for political change. It has, however, already been successful to a degree in pointing out the connection between powerlessness and what passes for lovemaking in many situations, and in verbalising the desire for love between equals, be they of the same or of different sexes.

4. Economic Justice

One of the most insistent demands of feminists, and the one that has recently received a fair bit of support from non-feminists, is the demand for economic justice, usually understood as equal pay for equal work. The problem with this concept is that men and women do not do equal work, and the economic gap between the sexes will not be reduced — and has, historically, not been reduced — with laws to this effect. This having been recognised by many feminists, the strategy has now been changed, and two quite different paths are being pursued: one strategy is focused on obtaining equal pay for work of equal value (that is, equal pay for dissimilar work that is judged to be equivalent) and the other focuses on the notion that that proportion of work done by women which is not being paid for at all, namely housework, needs to be recompensed if we ever wish to achieve economic justice between the sexes. The latter strategy is usually discussed under the heading of wages for housework. In the following, we shall briefly discuss the concepts of (a) equal pay for work of equal value, (b) wages for housework, and, as two alternative strategies, (c) wages for childcare or (d) a guaranteed annual income.

(a) Equal Pay for Work of Equal Value. The basic philosophy behind the concept of equal pay for work of equal value is the notion that job segregation by sex leads to differential pay, irrespective of the amount and quality of labour involved in each job. The intention of equal pay

for work of equal value legislation is to make incomparable jobs comparable by establishing universalistic criteria according to which the 'value' of jobs can be determined. Criteria discussed are usually (1) mental effort, (2) physical effort, (3) responsibility, (4) skill, (5) working conditions. Different jobs – e.g. truck driver and filing clerk – can then be compared according to those five criteria, and those jobs which are rated as equivalent in terms of their 'value-composition' must all be recompensed at the level of the best-paid job (one of the premises of this type of legislation is that it cannot be used as a tool to depress wages, it can serve only as a tool to raise wages, so that a lower-paid job that has been evaluated as of equal value with a higher-paid job must be raised to the higher-pay level, and not the higher-paid one reduced to the lower-pay level).

Difficulties in this approach are the establishment of criteria to decide what carries more responsibility – driving a bus with people inside or handling tax receipts – who does the rating, the restriction that comparisons can usually be made only within the same establishment, and that comparisons need to be made against a benchmark job, which has, historically, been defined by male role incumbents. The cost of implementing such policies, and, equally important, of enforcing compliance on the part of employers, is quite breathtaking.[1]

Criticisms of this approach maintain that unless control over job evaluation is in the hands of the workers, job evaluations for determining the 'value' of work will simply become another control mechanism of management; further, that 'value' is defined in male terms and is devoid of any notion of social value (which surely would rank childcare very highly, for example), that focusing on legislative concerns of minor import will divert energies from the more basic question of paying jobs for their social value, including at present unpaid jobs, and lastly, and probably most importantly, that pay scale determination through job evaluation would undermine collective bargaining through unions, and that in those places of work where women were strong enough to have input into work evaluations they would be strong enough to negotiate better pay settlements through a union.

Personally, I think that in spite of these possible problems equal pay for work of equal value legislation *is* of a limited utility, as long as it allows comparisons across establishments. If so, it could be one tool to protect the monetary interests of currently discriminated against women who are already in the labour market. However, there are two major drawbacks: it does nothing for women who work at socially useful tasks but who are not paid at all, and, if really successful, one of

the almost inevitable consequences of raising pay scales for female
workers to the degree that they would equal male pay scales would be
that certain types of jobs, for instance certain secretarial positions,
would be priced out of existence. That, in itself, need not necessarily be
a negative development, as long as one is prepared for it and opens up
other employment possibilities for women as some of the traditional
ones disappear. To neglect to plan for it might well have the undesirable consequence of diminishing employment opportunities for women.
As a protective mechanism for women in the paid labour force, the
legislation and enforcement of equal pay for work of equal value is
preferable to equal pay for equal work legislation, which demonstrably
does not have a very great effect although it is still necessary legislation.

The question of unpaid labour, and of enabling women who have
been out of the labour force for a prolonged period of time to re-enter
it, cannot be solved by such means. This is the point where the wages
for housework debate is of overriding importance.

(b) Wages for Housework. The most important ideas of people who
advocate wages for housework can be summarised as follows: All
women are housewives (e.g. 'All Women', 1975), whether married or
single, with or without children, straight or lesbian. The problem of
economic justice is misrepresented when it is seen as a problem of those
women on the labour market only, and when the solution to the wage-
lessness of women is presented in terms of finding a paid job, since
women have been doing productive work within the household for cen-
turies without being paid for this labour. The problem, then, is one of
money and not one of work; women work now, but more often than
not they are not being paid for their work, and if they are being paid
(for instance in a paying job) they are being paid too little. The productive work that goes on within the household is of a twofold nature:
'What we do at home is *produce and reproduce workers*: every day we
create and restore the capacity of others (and ourselves) to work, and
to be exploited' (Sweeney, 1977, p.104). In other words, women in the
household first restore the labour power of wage labourers by providing
them with food, clean shelter, clean clothing, and emotionally absorbing
the strains created by monotonous, alienating work, and second, they
produce the next generation of industrial workers, not only by giving
birth to them, but also by caring for them, and raising them for productive labour.

It appears that we freely donate all this work to our husbands and children out of love for them. In reality we are working for the same bosses, who are getting two workers for the price of one. Our lives are governed by the same work schedule as those we serve. When we cook dinner or when we 'make love' is determined by the factory time-clock. (Sweeney, 1977, p.104)

Therefore, housewives work for capital, but they work without a wage. Since work deserves a wage, housewives deserve a wage. This wage should be paid by capital (or, alternatively, the state). 'The state has a lot of money and all of it is ours. We want it back' (James, 1973, p.6, emphasised in the original).

The intention of the demand is not to keep women doing housework, albeit for pay, but to alter so drastically the social conditions in which housework is performed that it becomes a matter of choice whether women work inside or outside the home. ' . . . a housewife, if she wishes to destroy housework, must first gain that minimum leverage that a wage provides' (Allen, 1973, p.6). Wages for housework are seen, then, as the only means with which effectively to carry out a social revolution. ' . . . it is the only revolutionary perspective from a feminist viewpoint and ultimately the entire working class' (Frederici, 1975, p.2).

Feminists by no means agree on the desirability of wages for housework. Criticisms of this strategy centre around the following stated drawbacks:

1. Wages for housework not only does not question the basic division of labour by sex, it may even work towards maintaining this division of labour by sex; in other words, it will keep women in the house rather than integrate them into the larger society.
2. The cost of such a programme is such that one of two things would happen: either the full amount would be paid, in which case the state would go broke, or only a fraction of it would be paid, which would not greatly help women since it would leave them dependent upon men.
3. The conditions of housework (i.e. social isolation, monotony, overwork) would not be changed by a wage.
4. There is no concrete plan for action, it is an unrealistic demand.
5. Wages are paid out only under conditions of supervision. Therefore, wages for housework would create a condition of complete state supervision and licensing of private households, a nightmare of big brother's control that would thereby invade the last place where

autonomy and self-reliance can be practised. (For some of these criticisms see Malos, 1977, pp.63-6.)

Before discussing these criticisms, it is helpful to consider the various planes at which the wages for housework campaigns operate, since they do operate on more than one plane. The campaign (which consists of demonstrations, public rallies, and the production and wide dissemination of literature) can be understood on at least three different levels: as a programme for action, as an educational tool in the form of political rhetoric, and as an analytical tool that helps us better understand sex relations and the position of women in modern society. The relevance of the various criticisms depends largely on which level one sees the campaign as operating.

If the wages for housework campaign is understood as a programme for action, then the charge that it is an unrealistic plan becomes one of highest importance. I would agree that in the way it is at present phrased, with a wage claimed for every woman but not every adult, irrespective of marital, occupational and parental status, it is both unrealistic and unjustifiable. However, a careful reading of the material suggests that wages for housework proponents do not understand themselves as providing a detailed and realistic programme for action, they see themselves instead as engaging in political rhetoric with the aim of educating the masses and also as providing a tool for analysis that has previously been missing. Understood in this way, the charge that the programme — in so far as it has been elaborated — is unrealistic becomes an irrelevant criticism.

As an educational device, the wages for housework campaign has undoubtedly been somewhat successful. Although the 'masses' and the majority of social scientists tend as yet not to perceive unpaid work as work (the International Encyclopedia of Social Sciences defines 'work' explicitly as paid work, explicitly excluding the work done by housewives and by slaves, cf. Eichler, 1978), there has been a decided shift in the understanding of the nature of work among all feminists who have to struggle with the concept of wages for housework one way or the other. This is a process of redefinition which is one of the greatest achievements of the feminist movement to date. It can be expected that this process will eventually be reflected in the social sciences and that the definition of work as all work, whether paid or unpaid, will eventually be accepted by the majority of people.

It is on the third plane, that of the wages for housework concept as an analytical tool, that I have problems with the approach outlined, and that I see the criticisms as stated applicable.

In conventional analysis, work has been divided according to whether it was paid or not. The wages for housework approach rejects this as a useless and, worse, mystifying distinction and argues instead that all work, whether presently paid or unpaid, should be recognised as work and consequently paid. This reinterpretation has led to the possibility of discovering parallels between paid and unpaid work, and to recognition of the latent functions of housework for the maintenance of the economic system. On the other hand, by linking all unpaid housework with a demand for pay, it was necessary to imply that all such work is socially useful (not just privately useful, as, for instance, a hobby is useful in the sense that it is satisfying for the doer). This leads to what I see as an untenable position. In a special issue of *The Activist* (Spring 1975, vol. 15, nos. 1,2) which is devoted entirely to wages for housework, there is an interview with a Canadian housewife which illustrates the inherent contradiction in equating all unpaid labour with socially useful labour ('Portrait', 1975, pp.10-20). In the interview, the housewife, who keeps house for her husband, her two children, her brother and herself, details her work. An excerpt from the description of her continuous labours reads as follows. Every day she vacuums two rugs, dusts all furniture and moves all knick-knacks, does her fridge and stove, cooks (up to four meals), washes the kitchen floor, and takes care of her two children. Every third day she cuts the grass on a hundred foot lot, and weeds. Every second day she does (cleans?) the pool. At least once a week she does all her windows, inside and outside; every three months she takes all her drapes down and washes and irons them, plus she mops the ceilings. The walls are washed every three months, and every month she strips her floor of wax and rewaxes it. Four times a year she has a big cleaning in which all cupboards and drawers get cleaned out. Once a year she paints the outside of the house and all the ceilings. Every year she also paints all her bedroom furniture, to make it look nice, and twice a year she shampoos all her carpets and her upholstered furniture. In addition, she trims the trees, plants, harvests, freezes, cans, sews, irons, does the dishes, prepares for company which is 'a real big hassle. You have to go through all your good dishes, wash them all, iron your table cloths, get it really looking superb, and it takes you all day long just for doing all of this, and you don't get any of your other housework done. You have double to do all the next day and then you don't get càught up for a whole week' ('Portrait', 1975, p.11). There were other labours involved, but it tires me merely to contemplate this list of activities. Clearly, this woman works a great deal. To argue, however, that all this work is socially useful (or, by my standards, necessary) is another matter.

When arguing that housework deserves wages, the implication is that all housework is (a) necessary, that is it must be done in order to ensure the continued existence of our society, and (b) is socially useful, i.e. provides benefits for society in a direct or indirect way. The labours of this particular housewife benefit her family (presumably, although they might not notice if the knick-knacks were not moved every day), but the standards of cleanliness are clearly higher than those necessary for protecting members of the family from illness and are, therefore, perhaps appreciated but not necessary. I would argue that the first step towards liberation for this housewife would be to liberate herself from her own (or else her family's) standards of housekeeping, and to try to acquire friends who like to visit even though the table cloths are not newly pressed. Assuming, however, that she eliminated what might be called unnecessary work (and the dividing line would be debatable) and lowered standards drastically, a fair amount of work would still have to be done. Some of that work would be socially useful in the sense that it serves society, and some would be useful only for the members of the family.

In order to distinguish which portion of the remaining work would be socially useful, and which portion would be privately useful, we need to state some criterion for making such a distinction. To do so, it is helpful to separate analytically the various functions that are usually subsumed under the heading of 'housework'. We can distinguish between four primary functions in terms of the recipients of the services rendered: childcare, husbandcare, care for oneself and, where applicable, care for somebody else (in this case, a brother; in other cases, elderly parents or others). Together, these people need a fairly clean shelter, periodically cleaned clothes, continually prepared food, and a fair number of errands run. Everybody, in addition, needs emotional support, since the family is usually the primary group for social intimacy. However, this support is of a different nature from housekeeping, since the housewife herself is supposed to receive emotional support from others in exchange for giving them hers. Whether the exchange is always a fair one is a different question.

The functions, therefore, are roughly the same for each individual who is being served, but the recipients of the services are in different positions with respect to their ability to provide these services for themselves. One of the primary arguments of the wages for housework campaign is that the housewife ensures the workers (primarily male) are fit for another workday. It is, however, a fact that single workers continue to survive and continue to do productive work without the services of a housewife, although lack of a group of intimates may result in other problems. This is not a function of housekeeping services, but of a generalised human need of intimate interactions with other human beings.

If for some reason the housewife ceases to be capable or willing to render the customary housekeeping services, physically and mentally capable people are left to fend for themselves — our society does not acknowledge a social obligation to provide certain personal services for its physically and mentally capable members. On the other hand, if parents fail to look after their dependent children, society does recognise an obligation to look after the well-being of these people and will provide the means to ensure that these children do receive a minimum amount of care, necessary to their becoming independent and self-reliant members of society. In other words, the caring for children is, indeed, a social service that is rendered by housewives, mothers in general, and to a much lower degree by fathers, while looking after capable adult people is a service that is useful only to the recipients concerned.

Above, several criticisms of the wages for housework approach were listed. To this I would now like to add one more criticism. 'Wages for housework' constitute a means for a radical redistribution of income. That, indeed, is the appeal of the concept. One can make the assumption that such a redistribution would take place in a socialist state, in which case we are talking not only about redistribution of income but about a total political, social and economic revolution. If, on the other hand, we are assuming that the only major change we are discussing at this point of time is the wage for housework itself, then we must also assume that the monies from which such wages would be paid are tax monies. In that case, people in the labour force would subsidise people working at home. While this can be justified to the degree that the labour performed within the home is socially necessary labour (i.e. childcare), it cannot be justified where the labour performed within the home is only privately useful. Since everybody would be paying taxes, this would create a situation in which women and men in the labour force would support with their tax money the privilege of selected men to the full-time services of wives working for their comfort (assuming there are no dependent children), while the people in the labour force, both male and female, would not necessarily have such services themselves.

This, and other problems previously stated, could be overcome if we substituted the demand of 'wages for childcare' for the demand of wages for housework.

(c) Wages for Childcare. The basic proposal for wages for childcare is this. Every woman receives a wage for caring for her own children. This wage is based on considering childcare an eight-hours-a-day, five-days-a-week job, meaning that the caring that takes place and is necessary during the rest of the time is considered a parental obligation and is not paid for. A woman is paid this wage irrespective of her marital status, her labour force status, her own income from other sources (if any) and her husband's income (if any). The wage would be payable in full until such time that the child enters the public school system (either at age five or six) and after that it would be paid on a pro-rated basis, so that it covers only those periods during which the public does not already pay for childcare in the form of a public school system, namely to cover the unsupervised time during lunch hours and after school, plus those school holidays which are not statutory holidays. The administrative costs of such a programme would be minimal: in countries where some form of a baby bonus exists one would simply greatly augment the sum to be paid (so that it equals minimum wage for one child). The childcare wage would be taxable like any other income. In cases where the father is the major or only caretaker, the wage would be paid to him. The childcare wage would continue until such time as the child can reasonably be considered not to be in need of supervision, an arbitrary suggestion being by the age of 14 years.

A word of explanation is needed for the proposal that *all* women, irrespective of whether or not they are working on the labour market, receive this childcare wage. This is an extremely important aspect of the over-all proposal. At the present time many women, perhaps most, do not have the choice of devoting themselves full-time or part-time to childcare. Some of them must take paying jobs, even in the absence of good childcare facilities, in order to ensure family survival, whereas others cannot take on a part- or full-time paying job because they cannot arrange daycare as good as they themselves provide. By paying all mothers with small children a childcare wage we would, for the first time, give women a real option to accept full- or part-time employment or remain at home for a period of time, and, indeed, give the same option to fathers. Those women who decide to retain their other employment would have to hire child caretakers. Since everybody would know what the going rate for a full-time child caretaker is (defined as 8-hours-a-day, 5-days-a-week) the entire amount would be handed over to the other caretaker, from whom one could expect excellent care. Childcare almost certainly would become a desirable occupation for highly trained, highly committed personnel, since it could be well paying. Mothers who want to work half-days would, obviously, pay half-price for childcare services, etc. Mother and father could, if they so wished, work out a system whereby they could share the childcare, the childcare wages, and outside employment. Since the wage for raising one's own small children five days a week or other people's children for only a working week would be the same, women (or men) who desired to do this type of work could plan for it as a lifetime career. The problem of people having more children in order to get the wage is not a real one: at a worldwide level, fertility tends to decrease with increasing affluence. Since people could get the wage by raising other people's children during a working week, there would be no financial incentive to produce their own children.

Such a programme would acknowledge the importance for everyone of earning money. At the same time, it avoids the pitfalls that are present in the scheme of paying for housework, since it only pays for that portion of the 'housework' that is demonstrably of social value. (I would extend such a scheme also to pay for the care of other people who, for mental or physical reasons, are incapable of looking after themselves, such as mentally or physically handicapped people, or disabled elderly people.)

One of the criticisms made by critics of the concept of wages for housework is that it does not challenge the basic division of labour by sex. In a wages for childcare scheme, this problem would become unimportant, for two reasons. Occupational sex segregation is undesirable because women tend to have disproportionately low-paid, low-autonomy jobs. If women and men would work to a large degree at different jobs, with, however, the freedom to choose any job they want, and with equivalent pay and working conditions, personally I would not be concerned if we found that there still was some occupational sex segregation since it would be an expression of personal preferences rather than social coercion. It is, however, to be expected that if childcare were to be a well-paid job, men would want to work in it too, and the division of labour would be altered. At the family level, the division of labour by sex is undesirable because it involves asymmetrical, unreciprocated service of the woman to the man. This division of labour is upheld by the fiction that the man is the breadwinner and the wife his economic dependent. If she were paid for childcare (not for general household duties) the man would no longer be the breadwinner, and one of the rationales for the division of labour as it is would have been challenged. One could not expect drastic changes immediately with respect to the distribution of other households tasks, but the possibility of such change would be present. Lastly, women would be aware that their childcare wage is a full wage for a limited duration only — five or six years per child — and that, unless they want to make a career out of it, they will have to seek other employment later on. That, of course, is what many women do right now, only this life course tends to be un-prepared for since many women do not *plan* to return to the labour market after the last child has entered school, they simply *do* it. A limited-time childcare wage would make the need to plan for a second career obvious.

The conditions of housework, it was claimed, would not be changed if it were paid for: I would maintain that the conditions of childcare would be changed drastically if people were paid for it. Often, what child caretakers need is only an occasional break. With money at their disposal — earned by them, not granted by the bounty of their husbands — child caretakers could hire babysitters for short periods of time (a couple of hours) to refresh themselves in solitude or in adult company in whatever way they desired. Further, since childcare would be a real career option, training centres would almost certainly spring up, which would change the nature of childcare quite considerably.

Lastly, what about the fear of big brother watching our every move? Should incompetent mothers receive a wage for ruining their children? Should mothers be supervised in their jobs? It seems best to separate the question into two aspects: those people who are paid for caring for their own children, and those who are paid for caring for other people's children. It has long been an accepted notion that childcare workers should be trained, and people who work in daycare centres are usually licensed by the state. Considering the enormous social significance of their work, this is as it should be. Consequently, people who apply to be licensed as childcare workers should be obliged to undergo some rele-vant training and should receive a license which could be revoked in cases of proven incompetence. With money being available in this field, different forms of childcare would be certain to emerge: some of them could be variations of presently existing daycare centres, and others could be licensed homes in which women (or men) may look after up to a maximum of four pre-school children. Such places indeed would have to be licensed and should be licensed, and possibly periodically in-spected. This would create a whole new series of jobs — a highly desirable phenomenon in times of un- and underemployment.

What about mothers (or fathers) who raise their own pre-school children? We know that poverty in itself is perhaps the most detrimental environmental factor for children, and to the extent that need was alleviated by a childcare wage, the child would benefit directly. I would argue that all people, male and female, could only benefit from some childcare experience and knowledge, and that it would be highly desirable to train adolescents — e.g. through compulsory childcare courses in high school — to learn about childcare, thus better preparing them for their parental duties. This, in my opinion, would be a desirable development irrespective of any childcare wage. One could make the receipt of a childcare wage dependent on successful completion of a childcare course — a reasonable and feasible requirement. In cases of gross neglect and child abuse, children should be removed from their parental homes, as they are at present in most industrialised countries. Those mechanisms could simply be retained. Together a childcare course and more money should upgrade the quality of childcare. Children will certainly not be worse off in their own homes than they are now, and possibly better off. Mothers will certainly be better off as full-time or half-time mothers than they are now.

One of the greatest effects of a childcare wage would be an indirect one on the labour market: to the degree that occupational sex segregation is based on widespread unpaid housework, women would substantially better their bargaining position on the labour market, due to the simple factor that they would have an alternative in the form of childcare work to the low-paid, low-prestige, fairly undesirable jobs. A childcare wage would, therefore, drastically restructure not just familial relationships, but economic relationships throughout society.

There is, however, another mechanism with which such changes could be achieved, namely through a guaranteed annual income.

(d) Guaranteed Annual Income. The notion of a guaranteed annual income would provide every adult with a minimum income irrespective of other circumstances. The important aspect of such a scheme would have to be that individual adults receive such a guaranteed annual income, irrespective of sex and, even more important, irrespective of marital status. In other words, the purposes of such a programme would be defeated if the basic unit were the family rather than the individual. If adult individuals — say, of the age of 16, or 18 — were to receive a guaranteed annual income (again financed from taxes, and again a

radical means of income distribution) the asymmetrical dependency between housebound spouse and employed spouse would be largely overcome. Customs would have to change, of course, so that every member of a family who received some income would have to pay a portion of that income towards the maintenance of the joint residence, food costs, etc. This scheme would not necessarily solve the problem of providing sufficient income when there are several dependent children, but it would work towards that goal, and it would almost certainly improve relations between parents and children who are grown but still living at home, since it would give such 'children' financial independence from their parents, and thus make the living together optional on all sides. If one believes that people behave better when they want to live together rather than when they have no alternative but to live together, one can conclude that familial interactions would be almost certain to improve.

Feminism as a Form of Humanism

When discussing feminism as a socio-political movement, the question arises of what the role of men in such a movement can be. A man cannot be a feminist in the sense that a woman can. A white person cannot be a member of a black power movement in the sense that a black person can. One of the important aspects of liberation movements is the social network they provide for a redefinition of self at the collective as well as at the individual level. Were men successful in being part of the feminist movement in terms of participating in this process of collective and individual self-definition, or were whites successful in the process of the collective and individual self-definition of blacks, both movements would have failed to that degree. Liberation at the psychological level can only be achieved by the subjects concerned themselves.

On the other hand, everybody can participate in creating the preconditions for an abolition of the sexual double standard, by working for structural change which will allow women and men to meet as women and men without any power differential being involved. Such structural change involves a reconceptualisation and restructuring of the family, such that we cease to treat the family unit as the basic unit of society, and think of it instead as a set of interrelated individuals, who need to interact on a basis of equivalence. For men, accepting feminism therefore involves active cooperation in bringing about structural changes, and a redefinition and reallocation of their own roles that is no less drastic than it is for women. It affects the very core of our being, since being a man or woman is part of the most basic make-up of our personality. By redefining the social meaning of womanhood and manhood, we are redefining a basic aspect of ourselves.

In the sense that feminism seeks to accord an essential dignity to women as well as men, feminism is a form of humanism. A sexist humanist is not a humanist at all – it is a contradiction in terms. A sexist man cannot be a humanist, since to the degree that we deny the humanity of our fellow beings we lose that part of humanity ourselves, just as a social science that uses a double standard in the treatment of norms is a poor science that cannot adequately explain either female or male behaviour. Feminism and the fight against the double standard must be an integral part of our socio-political and scientific worlds.

Note

1. In 1975, the United States Equal Opportunity Employment Commission operated on a yearly budget of $55 million. In spite of this large budget, the average age of charges in inventory to be handled by the Commission were some two or more years old. Cf. Issie L. Jenkins, 'Equal Employment Opportunity in the United States: Title VII of the Civil Rights Act of 1964, as Amended its History and Operation', in Ontario Ministry of Labour, *Issues and Options: Equal Pay/ Equal Opportunity* (Toronto, 1978), pp.40-53.

References

'All Women are Housewives', *The Activist*, vol. 15, nos. 1,2 (1975), pp.6-7.

Allen, Priscilla. 'Wages for Housework Collection – Preface', *Women in Struggle No. 1, Wages for Housework* (n.p. 1973), pp. 5-7.

Boulding, Elise. *The Underside of History. A View of Women Through Time* (Boulder, Col., Westview Press, 1976).

Eichler, Margrit. 'The Double Standard as an Indicator of Sex-Status Differentials', *Atlantis*, vol. 3, no. 1 (Fall 1977), pp.1-21.

Eichler, Margrit. 'Women's Unpaid Labour', *Atlantis*, vol. 3, no.2 (Spring 1978), Part II, pp.52-61.

Frederici, Silvia. *Wages Against Housework* (Bristol, Power of Women Collective and the Falling Wall Press, 1975, pamphlet).

James, Selma. 'Interview with Selma James', *Guerilla*, vol. 3, no.29 (19 May 1973), pp.6-7.

Maccoby, Eleanor Emmons and Carol Nagy Jacklin. *The Psychology of Sex Differences* (Stanford, Stanford University Press, 1974).

Malos, Ellen. 'Housework and the Politics of Women's Liberation', *Socialist Review* 37 vol. 8, no.1 (Jan/Feb. 1978),

'Portrait of a Canadian Housewife', *The Activist*, vol. 15, nos.1,2 (1975), pp.10-20.

Sweeney, Pat, 'Wages for Housework: The Strategy for Women's Liberation', *Heresies*, no. 1 (1977), pp.104-6.

INDEX